Jules Renard

JOURNAL
1887–1910

TRANSLATED BY THEO CUFFE

SELECTED AND WITH AN INTRODUCTION
BY JULIAN BARNES

Jules Renard (1864–1910) was a French author and a member of the Académie Goncourt. A habitué of Parisian literary circles, he was the author of numerous novels and plays, among them *Carrot Top* and *Natural Histories*. His *Journal*, widely considered his masterpiece, was published posthumously between 1925 and 1927.

Theo Cuffe is known for his translations of classic French literature, including Voltaire's *Candide* and *Micromégas and Other Short Fictions*.

Julian Barnes is the Man Booker Prize–winning author of *The Sense of an Ending* and numerous other books.

JOURNAL
1887–1910

JULES RENARD

Translated from the French by
Theo Cuffe

Selected and with an Introduction by
Julian Barnes

PICADOR

New York

Picador
120 Broadway, New York 10271

Translation copyright © 2020 by Theo Cuffe
Selection and introduction copyright © 2020 by Julian Barnes
All rights reserved
Printed in the United States of America
This translation and selection first published in 2020 by Riverrun,
an imprint of Quercus Editions Ltd., Great Britain
Published in the United States by Picador
First American edition, 2022

Library of Congress Cataloging-in-Publication Data
Names: Renard, Jules, 1864–1910, author. | Cuffe, Theo, translator. | Barnes,
  Julian, editor.
Title: Journal 1887–1910 / Jules Renard ; translated from the French by
  Theo Cuffe ; selected and with an introduction by Julian Barnes.
Other titles: Journal, 1887–1910. English
Description: First American edition. | New York : Picador, 2022.
Identifiers: LCCN 2021049043 | ISBN 9780374260873 (paperback)
Subjects: LCSH: Renard, Jules, 1864–1910—Diaries. | Authors, French—
  19th century—Diaries. | Authors, French—20th century—Diaries. |
  LCGFT: Diaries.
Classification: LCC PQ2635.E48 Z46 2022 | DDC 848/.803—dc23/eng/20211110
LC record available at https://lccn.loc.gov/2021049043

Our books may be purchased in bulk for promotional, educational,
or business use. Please contact your local bookseller or the Macmillan
Corporate and Premium Sales Department at 1-800-221-7945, extension
5442, or by email at MacmillanSpecialMarkets@macmillan.com.

Picador® is a U.S. registered trademark and is used by Macmillan
Publishing Group, LLC, under license from Pan Books Limited.

For book club information, please visit facebook.com/picadorbookclub
or email marketing@picadorusa.com.

picadorusa.com • instagram.com/picador
twitter.com/picadorusa • facebook.com/picadorusa

1   3   5   7   9   10   8   6   4   2

Contents

Introduction	vii
1887	3
1888	7
1889	10
1890	20
1891	27
1892	37
1893	45
1894	59

CONTENTS

1895	80
1896	94
1897	116
1898	137
1899	157
1900	169
1901	188
1902	211
1903	236
1904	254
1905	274
1906	297
1907	323
1908	337
1909	358
1910	377

Introduction

Jules Renard (1864–1910) was born in the Nièvre, a poor, rather scrubby part of northern Burgundy. His father François, a peasant farmer who followed the plough, rose to become a builder and then mayor of the village, Chitry-les-Mines. He was taciturn, anti-clerical and rigidly truthful. Renard's mother, Rosa-Anne, was garrulous, theatrical and mendacious. The death of their first-born child so embittered François that he barely concerned himself with the next three: Amélie, Maurice and Jules. The father stopped speaking to the mother, and didn't address her directly for the next thirty years: if she came into the room he would pause in mid-sentence, wait for her to leave, and then continue the phrase. In this silent war Jules – whose sympathies lay with his father – was often used as go-between and *porte-parole*: once François sent him to ask Rosa-Anne if she would like a divorce. This was an unenviable role for any child, though an instructive one for a future writer.

Much of this upbringing finds its way into Renard's best-known work, *Poil de Carotte* (1894), which remained a standard text in French schools until the 1960s. In Chitry, many disliked this *roman à clef* by a red-headed village boy clever enough to escape to Paris, where he became sophisticated and wrote a book about a red-headed village boy which denounced his own mother. More broadly, Renard was decrying the whole sentimental, romantic image of childhood. Routine injustice and instinctive cruelty are the norms here; moments of pastoral sweetness the exception. Renard never indulges his child alter ego with retrospective self-pity, that emotion which makes many reworkings of childhood fake. For Renard, the child was 'a small, necessary animal', 'less human than a cat'. This remark comes from his masterpiece, the *Journal* which he kept from 1887 until six weeks before his death in 1910.

He began in a small way as a poet and journalist, then became a dramatist, a kind of novelist, and a private diarist. His material, themes and images overlap constantly from one genre to the next; so do his techniques. For instance, he imported into his novels the playscript's blunt way of setting out dialogue (thus avoiding fiction's repetitive he-said-she-said, followed by that over-familiar adverb to indicate tone). Renard was rightly proud of this innovation, until – as is often the fate of writers who imagine they have made a formal advance – he discovered its previous use in the writings of the Comtesse de Ségur. As well as being a happy overlapper, Renard was a cheerful recycler: he pillaged his occasional writings (and the *Journal*) for the nature notes he gathered as *Histoires Naturelles*. He also turned his prose writings into plays: so *Poil de Carotte* made his theatrical debut in 1900. At that time the stage was the equivalent of Hollywood today, a source of fame and money. But true success depended on a full-length play – and Renard's were only ever one or two acts long. In his *Journal*, he wondered sardonically if he would have remained a socialist if he had been able to manage a third act.

To the outward eye, Renard's life and career might seem almost entirely successful. At twenty-four he met and married the seventeen-year-old Marie Morneau, who brought with her a considerable dowry. Her sturdy and supportive nature allowed Jules as happy a marriage as his bearish, pessimistic self would permit; while her money allowed him to become co-founder and majority shareholder of the soon-fashionable magazine *Le Mercure de France*. They had two children, Jean-François and Julie-Marie, who feature in many clear-eyed but doting entries in the *Journal* (where they are rechristened Fantec and Baïe, while the Renard family name is changed to Lepic). His work was praised; he was awarded the Légion d'Honneur, whose ribbon he wore proudly, indeed aggressively, as several incidents in the *Journal* confirm; and he was elected to the Académie Goncourt. His social circle in Paris included writers, actors, poets, painters and politicians: Edmond Rostand, Alphonse Daudet, Edmond de Goncourt, Mallarmé, Rodin, Toulouse-Lautrec, Bonnard, Sarah Bernhardt, Jean Jaurès, Léon Blum, Gide, Claudel, Anatole France; among foreign celebrities he met Little Tich, Loie Fuller (on a bus), and even the exiled Oscar Wilde. His closest friends were the playwrights Tristan Bernard and Alfred Capus, and the actor Lucien Guitry (father of Sacha). In 1890 he served as second in a duel in which the opposing second was Gauguin. It would be easy to imagine Renard following the standard path of the provincial who succeeds in the capital: acquiring sophistication, charm and mistresses, while learning the arts of flattery and hypocrisy.

But, luckily for us as readers, his nature and principles forbade any easy satisfaction with life: as he self-fulfillingly told his *Journal* in 1894, 'Happy people have no talent.' And in 1899, 'If they built the House of Happiness, the largest room in it would be the waiting-room.' When *Histoires Naturelles* came out in 1896, the novelist and critic Lucien Muhlfield said to him, 'There's something of the priest about you, Renard. You can never forget your first communion. You are on the side of morality, chastity, duty.' Renard replied, 'That is correct. I am fed up with our literature, which is about nothing except cuckolds.' In the Paris of the day, Renard was – despite temptations noted in his diary – an incongruously faithful husband. In 1896, he wrote: 'At a sign from Sarah Bernhardt I would follow her to the ends of the earth – with my wife.' And when he was away from Marie, he wrote to her every day. They divided their lives between Paris and the Nièvre; in 1896 they rented, and later bought, a large presbytery in nearby Chaumot; in 1904 he took the sash as mayor of Chitry. He enjoyed exercising his civic duties, handing out school prizes and marrying the locals. In a letter to his wife, he wrote jauntily, 'My speech made the women cry. The bride gave me her cheeks to kiss, and even her mouth; it cost me twenty francs.' (In his diary, he seems to have been more truthful.) He also found the job could provoke a piquant bifurcation of response: 'As mayor, I am responsible for the upkeep of rural roads. As poet, I would prefer to see them neglected.'

Though capable of such geniality, Renard was known in both city and countryside as farouche and quarrelsome. One sophisticate called him a 'rustic cryptogram' – like one of those secret marks tramps used to chalk on outbuildings, decipherable only by other tramps. The harshness of the Nièvre, and of his strange, emotionally bleak upbringing, never left him. But if Renard was a fierce judge of human foible – especially Parisian foible – he was a fiercer judge of himself. The *Journal* is filled with self-rebuke and self-contempt. In November 1888, when his career has scarcely begun, he announces to himself 'You will come to nothing' – a lacerating judgement which he repeats five times in the same entry. He is dismissive of his own work: at best, he might amount to 'a pocket Maupassant' (and his opinion of the full-sized version was pretty mixed). His character and temperament disappoint him just as much; he doubts himself constantly, and falls into bitter depressions. His wit, his grasp of the dark comedy of human existence, and his need to put it all into words are the saving of him. Samuel Beckett, in a letter of January 1957, wrote of the *Journal* that, 'For me, it is as inexhaustible as Boswell.' Though Renard is much closer to the condensed pessimism of Beckett than the roistering ebullience of Boswell.

Shuttling between Paris and the Nièvre was necessary for his sanity and sense of proportion. Also for his writing: 'It is in the middle of town,' he noted in his first year of diary-keeping, 'that one writes one's best pages about the country.' And Renard was very, very French. It was not that France was in any way perfect; just that it was self-evidently superior to other countries. He also knew, instinctively, that French literature was the only literature worth being interested in. Heine, Dickens and Thackeray are all brutally dismissed. Ibsen is admired; but 'foreign novels, even the Russians, even Tolstoy, I find intolerable'. So too was Shakespeare, who disappointed him time after time, up until 1906, when first seeing and then reading *Julius Caesar* made him realize that the Englishman was 'less literary ... but more human' than Victor Hugo; and that whereas Hugo left us with an image burning in our mind, Shakespeare left us with 'the truth, the muscles and the blood of truth'. Hugo being Renard's highest literary god, this is extravagant praise. However – Shakespeare apart – the British are treated with little but mockery in the *Journal*; and Renard fails to rise above the standard French view of his time that Englishwomen were comically unattractive.

He is a man of firm, often harsh, opinions and swift judgement. In 1894 he tastes a banana for the first time, and swears it will definitely be the last. He feels much the same about classical music: *Pelléas et Mélisande* is a 'sombre bore', its plot 'puerile'; *Die Walküre* not just boring but made of cardboard and containing 'not a moment of real emotion or beauty'. When Ravel proposes setting some of the *Histoires Naturelles* to music, Renard is simply baffled: he cannot see the point of it, and declines to go to the premiere, sending his wife and daughter in his place. And though three of the greatest artist-illustrators of the day – Bonnard, Lautrec and Vallotton – decorated his texts, he doesn't seem to have been markedly grateful or interested. He was generally more tolerant of painting than of music: he admired Lautrec and Renoir, but found Cézanne 'barbarous' and Monet's waterlilies 'girly'. Perhaps this was not so much combative philistinism as a robust admission of his own areas of non-response. And he did make one wonderful note about painting, on 8 January 1908: 'When I am in front of a picture, it speaks better than I do.'

I said that he was 'a kind of novelist'. He was a great observer of life, but a weak inventor of it, and he raised this inaptitude to a matter of principle. He maintained that the imagination, far from being a means of accessing the truth, was truth's very opposite; indeed, it was an 'odious' corruptor of the truth. Hence all his fictional and dramatic writings were closely autobiographical. But it went beyond this: Renard perceived that the novel, as understood for most of the nineteenth century, was in a state of crisis, if not actually dead as a genre. In 1891 he noted that 'the form of the novel is finished'. And the following year: 'The new system for writing a novel is not to write a novel.' In other words, the great descriptive and analytical project, starring Flaubert, Maupassant, Goncourt and Zola, which had dominated the second half of the century, had used up the world as it was, and left nothing for fiction to do. The only way forward, Renard concluded, was through compression, annotation, pointillism. Allied to this was a further scepticism: about the integrity of the personality, that staple belief of the old novelists. Just after his twenty-eighth birthday, Renard announced that the personality was 'discontinuous'. A few years later: 'There is no unity; there is only discontinuity.' Sartre, in a rather grand and somewhat grudging tribute to the *Journal*, acclaimed Renard's dilemma more than the solution to it: 'He is at the origin of many more modern attempts to seize the essence of the single thing'; and 'If he is where modern literature begins, it is because he had the vague sense of a domain which he forbade himself to enter.' In this view, the *Journal* is not just a rich, strange, characterful collection of private jottings, but an attempt to make a new form of writing.

André Gide, whose own journal overlaps for many years with Renard's, complained (perhaps rivalrously) that the latter's was 'not a river but a distillery'; though he subsequently admitted to reading it 'with rapture'. Do you want a distillery or a river? Life rendered in a few drops of the hard stuff, or as a litre of Normandy cider? These are choices for the reader. The writer has little control over personal temperament, none over the historical moment, and is only partly in charge of his or her own aesthetic. Renard admitted that if he had been born twenty or thirty years earlier, he would inevitably have written naturalistic novels like everyone else. Instead, distillation became Renard's aesthetic response to the literature that had gone before, and the fullest expression of his often unexpressive nature. In 1898, he noted: 'It may be said of almost all works of literature that they are too long.' Ironically, this remark comes four-tenths of the way through the thirteen-hundred-page *Journal*, which would have been half as long again had Renard's widow and her literary advisor not cut a third. Nor did she just edit text: in the offices of the *Journal*'s original publishers, she 'triumphantly' announced, 'Now you don't need to worry any more – we've burnt the lot.' Only a single facsimile page of the manuscript has survived.

Renard attends to the natural world with intense precision, describing it with an entirely unsentimental admiration. He attends to the sophisticated human world with the same precision, describing it with scepticism and irony. The peasant, lying midway between these two worlds – 'A peasant is a tree trunk that moves' – is described with a kind of wondering irony. But Renard fully understood, as many did not, the nature and function of irony. On 26 December 1899, just as the century which would most need it was about to begin, he wrote: 'Irony does not dry up the grass; it merely burns off the weeds.' He considered the phrase 'human stupidity' a pleonasm, since only humans are capable of stupidity; animals remain merely themselves, no more capable of stupidity than of hypocrisy. 'It is all beautiful,' he wrote. 'One must write about a pig as about a flower.' He compared his own approach to nature with that of Buffon, the great eighteenth-century naturalist (and a *grand seigneur* to Renard's country lad): 'Buffon described animals in such a way as to please humans. Whereas I want to please the animals themselves. I would like my book, if they could read it, to make them smile.' But it would be a smile in recognition of observed truth. There are no Jemima Puddleducks and flopsy bunnies in Renard's world; or rather, bunnies are only flopsy when in the mouth of a gun dog. Here, animals are given their full reality and dignity, strangeness and purpose. Buffon and other traditionalists also liked to impose on the natural world a hierarchy parallel to the hierarchies of human society: thus the horse is nobler than the donkey, the swan posher than the goose. Renard, by contrast, is a socialist among the animals. He looks at disregarded or unattractive beasts with understanding; he rehabilitates the bat, and thinks the pig's squalor is our fault rather than its. Indeed, the pig rides very high in Renard's estimation: the only thing it can't do, he notes, is make its own black pudding. And – perhaps surprisingly – Renard doesn't stop taking nature notes during his Paris months: he is often at the zoo, studying the exotic imported fauna. The giraffe and the zebu provoke the same wry rapture as a poolful of croaking frogs in the Nièvre.

But the natural world, however beautiful and unstupid, is also a place of constant danger and death, with the greatest predator being man himself. I remember a Breton peasant-priest telling me, decades ago, 'It's strange, Monsieur Barnes, I love animals, but I kill them.' He said it as if it were a paradox only God could resolve. Renard was similarly poised between entranced admiration for the birds and beasts, and a routine shooting of them. Hare and partridge fell regularly to his gun (he imagines himself in the afterlife being savagely pecked by every partridge he has shot during his time on earth). But even a committed countryman can sometimes tire of slaughter. Renard brought his own shooting season to a close on 1 September 1904. He had seen a lark fly up, then perch on a clod of earth. 'It's dangerous to have a gun. So I shoot, not because I want to kill the bird, but just to see what would happen.' Inevitably, he doesn't miss, and 'what happens' is the lark lying on the ground leaking blood, feet waving, beak opening and closing. 'I have torn up my hunting permit and hung my shotgun from a nail on the wall.'

Life, and death – and beyond them, perhaps God? In literature, Renard believed in 'the truth' rather than 'the imagination'. In politics, he was a socialist and a Dreyfusard who saw in both Paris and the Nièvre the great injustices inflicted by the rich and powerful on the poor and weak. In religion he was as anti-clerical as his father, who was the first person to be buried in Chitry cemetery without benefit of clergy. There was nothing of the mystic about Jules Renard; nor did his fascination with the natural world lead him into any kind of pantheism. The *Journal* is full of brilliant, sardonic witticisms about God: 'I don't know if He exists, but it would be better for His reputation if He did not'; 'God does not believe in our God'; 'Yes, God exists, but He knows no more about it than we do'; 'I'm happy to believe anything you suggest, but the justice of this world doesn't exactly reassure me about the justice of the next. I fear God will just carry on blundering: He'll welcome the wicked into Heaven, and boot the good down into Hell.' And yet, and yet . . . The true sceptic must also be sceptical about his scepticism. Though repelled by the complacent certainties of the pious (often epitomized in his own sister), and by the tyranny of parish priests over the credulous and ill-educated, Renard cannot entirely chase away the spectre, the possibility of God – not least given the feebleness of human knowledge. 'I don't understand life, but it's not impossible that God does'; 'Is the fact that God is incomprehensible really the strongest argument for His existence?' For Renard, if you took away the church, then the whole thing might become more plausible: 'In my church, there is no vaulted roof between me and Heaven.'

And that leaves death, with which Renard has a close familiarity. In 1897 his father, knowing or at least believing himself to be incurably ill, locks himself in his bedroom and uses a walking stick to fire both barrels of his shotgun into his abdomen. Jules admires the deed, and notes, 'On the whole, this death has added to my sense of pride.' Three years later, his brother Maurice, a seemingly healthy thirty-seven-year-old clerk of works in the Highways Department, collapses in his Paris office and is dead by the time Jules arrives. He reflects: 'All I feel is a kind of fury at death and its imbecile tricks.' And in August 1909, his mother falls backwards – whether by accident or design – into the village well at Chitry. He calls the death 'unfathomable', and concludes, 'Death is no artist.' These calamities are, however, accompanied by intrusive comic moments which only someone like Renard would record. When he gets the emergency summons to his father, his first decision is to pump up his bicycle tyres. When he sees his brother's corpse, he notices that the head has been placed on a Paris telephone directory, along the fore-edge of which is an advertisement printed in black; he tries to read it from a respectful, seated distance. And when, attempting to rescue his mother from the well, he steps into the bucket to be lowered down, he can't help observing that his boots seem ridiculously long and are bending up at the ends like fish in a pail.

In January 1902, Renard had written: 'Please, God, don't make me die too quickly! I shouldn't mind seeing how I die.' In March

1909 he was diagnosed with emphysema and arteriosclerosis. He began a life *au lit et au lait* (bed and milk – two and a half litres a day). God gave him just over a year to watch himself die. He said: 'Now that I am mortally ill, I should like to make a few profound, historical utterances, which my friends will subsequently repeat; but then I get too overexcited.' He said: 'Don't worry! Those of us who fear death always try to die as stylishly as possible.' He said: 'Paradise does not exist, but we must nevertheless strive to be worthy of its existence.' And so he continued, scrupulous, witty and sceptical, until the end came in Paris on 22 May 1910. He was buried at Chitry four days later, without benefit of clergy, just like his father and brother before him. At his writerly request, no words were spoken over his body.

JULIAN BARNES

JOURNAL
1887–1910

1887

[Undated.]

I have a horror of stories with a realistic setting. Which is no doubt why I like travel books so much, being 'no good' at geography; in which the places described seem merely vague regions of imagination or reverie; as if they did not exist.

Who knows if each event is not the realization of a dream we have had, or someone else has had, which we can no longer recall, which did not even happen to us.

Talent is about quantity. Talent does not write one page: it writes three hundred. There is no plot which an ordinary intelligence could not think up – no sentence, however lovely, that a novice could not produce. What is needed is to pick up the pen, rule the paper, patiently fill the lines. The strong do not hesitate. They settle in, they sweat it out, they keep going to the end. They run out of ink, they use up all the paper. That is the only difference between men of talent and the rest, the slackers who will never make a start. In literature, there are only beasts of burden. The biggest of these are the geniuses – those who slog for eighteen hours a day without tiring. Fame is a daily struggle.

20 June.

The nostalgia we feel for countries we have never visited is perhaps merely the memory of regions travelled and voyages undertaken in former lives.

22 July.

The sea, like a great artist, kills for the sake of killing, and casts the remains on the rocks with scorn.

9 August. Seaside.

The sea rises, takes the rocks one by one, drowns this one, licks that one, foams all over this other one, and through its bottle-green element it shows them to be so many fantastical petrified monsters with hair of kelp.

Crabs: marching pebbles.

On the white sand, a lighthouse rises up like a coffee-flavoured *parfait* on a tablecloth.

17 September.

A scrupulous inexactness.

21 October.

How to raise the boulangerie to the level of a national institution: mandatory free bread.

23 October.

In my case, an almost constant need to speak ill of others, and no interest whatsoever in doing them ill.

28 October.

How peculiar, the world of dreams! Thoughts, inner speech, deep down, crowding and swarming together. An entire little world rushes into being before the wake-up call – which is its end, its particular death.

29 October.

Those moments when you want to tell the sluggard sun: 'Time's up! Rise and shine!'

31 October.

We often wish we could exchange our actual family for a literary equivalent of our own choosing, to be able to say to this or that author of a page which has moved us: 'Brother.'

3 November.

To lie in wait for one's mind, pen raised, ready to spear the slightest thought as it surfaces.

To encounter other egoists astounds us, as though we alone had the right to be selfish and avid for life.

14 November.

Sometimes everything around me seems so diffuse, so tremulous, so flimsy, that I think of this world only as the mirage of a world to come: its projection. We seem always to be far from the forest; and though the great trees already cast their shadow over us, there is still a long way to go before we walk beneath their foliage.

25 November.

It is in the middle of town that one writes one's best pages about the country.

13 December.

To faint is to drown in air. To drown is to faint in water.

1888

February.

A word so delicious that one wishes it had cheeks, so as to kiss them.

9 October.

A letter from my father that saddened me. No mention of my *Crime de Village* stories – not a word. Another vanity I shall have to rid myself of.

11 November.

Rational thought bears as much relation to reality as geometry to architecture. It is pure folly to try and apply its procedures to your daily life, just as it would be unscientific to assume that there are straight lines in nature.

15 November.

A friend is like a suit of clothes. You must replace it before it becomes too worn. Otherwise it is you who are replaced.

A thought written down is dead. It was alive. It lives no longer. Like a flower. Writing it down has made it artificial, that is to say, changeless.

23 November.

The poet should do more than dream: he should observe. I am convinced that this is how poetry will renew itself. It needs a transformation analogous to that which has taken place with the novel. Who would believe that we are still under the yoke of an ancient mythology! What point is there in pretending that the tree is inhabited by a faun? It is inhabited by itself. The tree lives: it is this that requires belief. A plant has a soul. A leaf is not what our vanity would prefer it to be. We speak of dead leaves, but we don't really believe that they die. What is the point of creating life to one side of life? Fauns, you've had your day: it is with the tree itself that the poet now wishes to confer.

You will amount to nothing. However hard you try, you will amount to nothing. You may understand the greatest poets, the greatest prose, but although we pretend that to understand is to be on equal terms, you will be to them as a dwarf to giants.

You work every day. You take life seriously. You believe fervently in your art. Your consumption of women is modest. And you will amount to nothing.

You have no money worries, no need to work for a living. So here you are, free, and your time is your own. You have only to wish. But you lack the force.

You will amount to nothing. Weep, lose your temper, hold your head in your hands, hope, despair, go back to your desk, roll your boulder uphill. You will amount to nothing.

Your head has an odd shape, as if sculpted with great strokes of the chisel, almost like a man of genius. Your brow catches the light, almost like Socrates. Phrenologically speaking, you are of a type, like Cromwell, Napoleon and many others, and yet you will amount to nothing. So why this waste of effort, of favourable endowments, if you are destined to come to nothing?

29 December.

How many people, after resolving to commit suicide, have settled instead for tearing up their photograph?

1889

15 January.

One thing I am always astounded by: the universal admiration of the literary world for Heinrich Heine. I can make nothing of this German who tried – a big mistake – to pass himself off as French. His *Lyrisches Intermezzo* is the work of a novice straining after poetic effects.

17 January.

The man of science generalizes, the artist particularizes.

18 January.

'Soul' – without any doubt the word that has been responsible for the greatest number of idiocies. When one reflects that in the eighteenth century men of sense, in the name of Descartes, refused to allow animals a soul. Apart from the absurdity of refusing to allow other creatures something of which man himself has not the slightest idea, you might as well claim that the nightingale has no voice, but carries in its beak a small whistle, cleverly fashioned, purchased from Pan or some other trinket-merchant of the hedgerows.

23 January.

Countrymen, so-called, almost never mention the countryside.

25 January.

It should be forbidden, on pain of a fine or even imprisonment, for a modern author to borrow a comparison from mythology, or to mention harps, lyres, muses or swans. Storks are another matter.

2 February.

One can well believe that the eyes of the newborn, eyes that see nothing and into which it is difficult to look – eyes without whites, deep and expressionless – retain a little of the abyss from whence they come.

26 February.

'Madame,' says the older matron to the younger woman, by way of reassurance: 'Don't worry: giving birth feels like doing a big poo.'

12 March.

Words of a mother-in-law.
'Yes, Maman.'
'In the first place, I am not your Maman, and I have no use for your dainty manners.'

She used to forget to set a place at table for her daughter-in-law, or would hand her a dirty fork, or, wiping the table, would deliberately leave crumbs in front of her. Or would even go so far as to heap everyone else's crumbs in front of her. No opportunity for annoyance was too small.

She could be heard muttering that 'nothing is right, ever since this stranger came to the house'. And this stranger was the wife of her son. Her fury was further inflamed by the affection shown to the young woman by her father-in-law. If they met in the hallway she would draw herself together, press her arms against her sides and flatten herself against the wall, as though afraid of being contaminated. Or she would heave great sighs, declaring that if grief really killed she would be dead already. She would even spit on the ground to express her chagrin. [. . .]

She had her changes of mood, it is true. And when they happened they were very touching.

'My dear, sweet girl, what can I do for you? Don't mind me – I am as fond of you as my own daughter. Here, let me fill your basin. Let me do the heavy work. Your hands are too white for that.'

Suddenly, her expression would turn nasty: 'Am I the maid-of-all-work?'

And, in her bedroom, she would separate photographs of her children from those of her daughter-in-law, leaving her isolated, left out, and no doubt sorely vexed.

[*Marginal note added by Renard when he re-read his* Journal *in 1906: 'It was this attitude towards my wife which provoked me to write* Poil de Carotte.*'*]

1889

29 March.

Tears are the most foolish form of exaggeration. As exasperating as a dripping tap.

31 March.

I know a great strapping lad, twenty-four years old, runs three farms, treats his men harshly but loves his cattle, who at any moment is covering a bullock or stallion, rolls up his sleeves and gets stuck into helping his cows to calve, pushes back the uterus of his ewe when it drops, knows all the tricks of his trade – but who says to my wife, with a shy and embarrassed air: 'Don't tell Maman I am reading Zola's *La Terre*.'

6 April.

Huysmans, always worrying about the state of his characters' teeth.

8 April.

The married man is to the boy as the finished copy to an unbound folio.

10 April.

Horror of the bourgeoisie is bourgeois.

21 May.

'So what is Jules doing?'
'He is working.'
'I can see that he is working. But at what?'
'At his book, as I told you.'
'It takes him this long to copy out a book?'
'He is not copying it, he's making it up.'
'Making it up! So it's not true, then, what gets written in books?'

28 May.

The friendship of a true man of letters would be a real boon. It is a pity that those whose good graces one seeks are always dead.

14 June.

Do we have a destiny? Are we free? What a bore not to know. And what a bore were we to know!

9 July.

Every girl contains a grandmother.

9 August.

A dog coming downstairs: like the descent of a stuffed mattress.

1889

16 August.

When a train goes onto the turntable, the carriages sound like they have hiccups.

28 August.

It's enough to make you despair: to read everything and remember nothing! For one forgets everything. Do your damnedest, it all vanishes. Here and there a few scraps remain, fragile as those puffs of smoke which show that a train has passed.

30 August.

Say what you like: up to a certain age – I have yet to discover what age – there is no pleasure in talking to a woman you cannot imagine as a mistress.

1 September.

Mademoiselle Blanche was a cashier in the washrooms during the Universal Exposition of 1878. You paid 5 sous, and 10 sous for a cubicle with a washbasin. She used to announce the price-list with pride, and we assume – faced with the fabulous enormity of the entry fees – that they must have smelt less bad than in our day, when such places of confinement are of a derisory cheapness. Besides, why the drop in prices? Either you need to go or you don't need to go, no?

6 September.

I envy painters. Their control of their public. This morning I watched Monsieur Béraud in the Palais des Machines [at the Exposition Universelle] ... His canvas was in front of him. It was taking shape. Presided over by Monsieur Béraud's grey hat, on top of the easel. The artist spreads a little paint on his palette, applies it delicately, takes a step back, smiles, remarks on the stubbornness of the subject and tells me that he would like to start again from scratch. What is more, he has a little rod in his hand, with which now and then he makes an alarming swishing sound. He indicates a luminous point, in the background, a difficult passage to disentangle. How do you expect a member of the public to respond to this composition? He is defeated in advance. But his vanity is at stake, led by the nose of his stupidity. He does not grasp what he is looking at, of course, but if he shows incomprehension, his neighbour will notice: it is in his interest to seem in the know. So now he is an expert, and ventures some bland opinion, scanning the picture from right to left as he does so. At this point the painter smiles. The painter has smiled! The public is gripped. The public will talk about the smile and about the painting, but mostly about the smile. The opinion that was ventured was so clearly on the mark!

The painter dominates the idle onlookers by his presence and by his baton. And then, to watch him at work. Now there's real work!

A writer burns the midnight oil in order to finish a book. A member of the public purchases it for a few francs. He opens it at home, and quite alone, mark you, without any trepidation. He can throw it in the wastepaper basket if he likes – and when he likes. He is a free agent. He fears neither his neighbour nor the painter's menacing rod. He can be stupid at his leisure. With a single tearing movement he can destroy the book, which cost only a few francs – like a governess who, unobserved, grips the chair of a baby who cries too much, and says under her breath: 'You little monster.'

I envy painters.

8 September.

Mme Barat, having informed us that she adores her husband, tells us that he wears stockings, and garters, and that in summer he insists on having small shorts in blue canvas, like the culottes worn by the Swiss. It is she who runs them up for him; he likes them in blue: there is no arguing with him. She concludes with: 'Oh well – old husbands and their manias!'

18 September.

What has not yet been written: a contemporary work on rural life.

25 September.

I read novel upon novel, I stuff myself with them, I am bloated with them, up to my neck in them – purely so as to disgust myself with their commonplaces, their repetitions, their conventions, their all too predictable tricks. And so that I may do otherwise.

30 September.

In the fencing-hall, a huddle of marquises and counts. They lived off their names as others live off their labour. They affect me powerfully. A plebeian, the son of a peasant, I regard them all as imbeciles. But they impress me, and when I pass in front of their sad anatomies, in varying states of undress, I timidly beg their forgiveness.

6 October.

One day they'll put a phonograph inside our clocks. Instead of striking the hour, a voice will say: 'Five o'clock' – 'Eight o'clock.' We will say: 'You're slow' – 'You're fast.' We shall talk to Time, and Time will stop for a chat, like a garrulous concierge or shopkeeper's assistant.

9 October.

'I am vain,' I say, and it is true – not least because I am so fond of saying it.

21 October.

When I hold a woman in my arms, I am perfectly aware that even now I am engaged in literature. I say this or that to her because I am supposed to, and because it is literary. Even here, it is impossible for me to be natural. I have no knowledge of English, but I would find it easier to say 'I love you' in English than spontaneously in my native tongue.

This evening, memories are using my brain as their tambourine.

25 November.

I like people – more or less – depending on whether they furnish me with raw material.

4 December.

Tailors are droll. 'Monsieur,' says one of them, trying out various overcoat collars, 'we stock all necks.'

6 December.

A man who learns of the death of his mistress, in the presence of his wife, and, unable to give vent to his grief, expresses it in a few words: 'I am widowed.'

26 December.

That intense sensation which makes you take hold of a sentence as though it were a weapon.

1890

2 January.

You can be a poet and wear your hair short.
You can be a poet and pay your rent.
Even though you are a poet, you can sleep with your wife.
A poet is even allowed, now and then, to write proper French.

28 January.

The bourgeoisie is other people.

1 February.

Write a novel in which you kill off a contemporary figure before his time.

14 February.

Avid to know everything, and keep abreast, I have acquired a taste for very short books, easy to read, large type with a lot of white space – so that I can toss them into my bookcase, one after another, and move on to the next.

17 February.

Look for the ridiculous in everything and you will find it.

18 February.

Victor Hugo and the rest of them see the child as an angel. What needs to be seen is the savage, the wild animal. The literature of childhood can only be renewed if we see the world through their eyes. You have to smash the sugar-stick child which all the sentimental Droz types have until now given the public to suck on. A child is a small, necessary animal. Less human than a cat. Not the child who masters language, but the child who sinks his claws into everything tender that comes his way. The endless concern of the parent is to get him to retract them.

20 February.

That questing and circular look with which an actor, even in the midst of the deepest concentration, seeks to reassure himself that he is being looked at, that he is being noticed.

21 February.

So much the worse for me, alas, that music bores me. Of painting I know nothing, and sculpture gives me as much pleasure as a wax dummy at the hairdresser's. Behold! she lives, she turns slowly on her pedestal, she bows and rises, just like a judge in court, lifting and lowering her false wig with mechanical regularity.

Sometimes it is the opinion of a critic we dislike that makes us like the book that is under attack.

13 March.

As useless for a people to fear war as for the individual to fear death.

17 March.

I am going through an ugly phase. All books disgust me. I do nothing. I am more than ever aware that I serve no purpose. I feel that I will never get anywhere; and the lines I write seem puerile, ridiculous and, above all, entirely pointless. How to get out of this fix? There is one expedient: hypocrisy. I shut myself away for hours, and everyone thinks I am working. Some of them feel sorry for me, perhaps; others admire me; as for myself, I get bored, I yawn, my eyes full of jaundiced reflections from the yellow of the bookcase. I have a wife who is gentle and strong, full of life, and an infant who would take prizes in a baby contest, yet I have not the strength of purpose to enjoy any of it. I know that this mood will pass. I will have new hopes, new convictions, I will redouble the attack. If only these confessions served some purpose – if one day I became a psychologist of renown, a Paul Bourget! But I do not believe there is enough life in me. I shall die before my time, or give up and become a drunkard of daydreams. Better to break stones, plough fields. Am I to waste my life, long or short, saying, 'You'd be better doing something else'? Why this see-sawing of the soul, this pitching and rolling, coming and going of enthusiasms? Our hopes are like the tides: when they withdraw they leave exposed a sickening mess of debris, revolting shells and crabs, stinking mental crabs washed up on the beach, which now scuttle sideways to catch up with the sea. How sterile, the life of a writer who doesn't succeed! Clearly I am intelligent, more intelligent than many others. The proof: that I can read *La Tentation de saint Antoine* without falling asleep. But this intelligence is like water running off, unseen, unused, in a spot where no one has yet thought to build a mill. Yes, that is it: I have not yet found my mill. Shall I ever find it?

17 April.

Dumas *père et fils*: they overturned the economic model – the first was the prodigal, the second the miser.

30 April.

Metempsychosis with added fertilizer: the soul of Bismarck passing into the heart of a sensitive plant.

5 May.

'My fear when I got married (I had only one fear),' says the young woman, 'was that I might need to go to the toilet during the nuptial blessing.'

11 May.

What I look for above all in a novel are curiosities of expression. Which is to say that novels in translation – even Russians, even Tolstoy – I find intolerable.

28 May.

To believe that the human is merely what is peculiar to ourselves, there lies the big mistake.

13 June.

When I make a joke, I watch the maid out of the corner of my eye to see if she is laughing.

21 June.

The boat advances behind its sails like an antique warrior behind his shield.

It is in the theatre above all that each individual is responsible for his actions.

18 July.

An exotic plant opening like a fan made of razors.

12 August.

Merimée is perhaps the writer who will endure longest. Because he relies less than anyone else on images, which cause a style to date. Posterity will belong to the dry writers, to the constipated among us.

5 September.

The day is fast approaching when kites in the sky will be enlisted as aids to photography.

24 September.

We are ignorant of the Beyond, because ignorance is the *sine qua non* of our existence here. Just as ice cannot know fire except by melting, by vanishing.

29 November.

It would be a shame to waste, without producing a masterpiece, the time during which one still has faith in literature: given that it will not last.

10 December.

Met Alphonse Daudet this morning. Bonnetain was there. Daudet got to his feet, examined me in the light, and said: 'I recognize Poil de Carotte.' A fine head, such as one sees in shop windows, beard touched here and there with grey. A

Provençal, but much mellowed, old before his time, already crippled, walking with the help of a rubber-tipped cane. He praised me extravagantly. I did not know what to reply. Should I address him as 'Monsieur', or 'Cher Maître'? His conversation touched on everything, without any display of wit, but with breadth, and good sense.

He said: 'The first and only time I tried to play the bagpipes was with some female cousins, and I farted loudly; yes, trying to swell my poor cheeks, I let out a gigantic fart. I am reminded of this sorry episode by the young scribblers of today.'

1891

10 January.

Whatever our integrity, as authors, we can still be classified as thieves.

13 February.

Ah, the literary life . . . I dropped by Lemerre's bookshop this evening. I don't go there often, out of timidity. No copies of *Sourires pincés* on display. Suddenly the imbecilic notion flashed across my mind that the 1,000 copies had perhaps sold out. When I entered, my heart was beating a little faster.

Lemerre did not even recognize me.

24 February.

A trembling signature, afraid to speak its name.

25 February.

This morning, a good conversation with Alphonse Daudet, for an hour and a half. He seemed to be in less pain, walked almost naturally, was in good spirits. [. . .]

'Did you know Victor Hugo?'

'Yes, I dined with him often. He thought I was a joker. I drank almost as much as he, but I always declined to present him with any of my books. I told him, "You will not read them, cher Maître, and you will get one of your female courtiers to write to me in your place." I obstinately kept up this persona, and Hugo died without knowing me. Mme Daudet was like a little girl at the Hugo table. She dared not speak, no doubt fearful of being confused with the pretentious bluestockings who surrounded the master. At bottom, her timidity was pride. I go every Sunday to visit [Jules] de Goncourt. It is hard for me, but I do it. He is so alone, no entourage left! It is I who founded his *Grenier*. [. . .]

'I have taken to writing whatever comes into my head. A thought, I capture it in flight, no matter how morbid or murderous. It is clear that these thoughts do not always represent who I am. We are not responsible for the things which fill our heads. We can chase away what is immoral or absurd, but we cannot prevent it from paying a call.

'One day, I had written that only our earliest impressions are ineffaceable. The rest is mere repetition, a matter of habit. The next day, I found this page scored with nail marks: Mme Daudet had read it, a little inquisitively, and it seems she had reasoned thus: "So he has said 'I love you' to other women before me. I came after them. How sincere then are his words of love?"

'Life is a box of implements which prick and wound us. At every moment we have blood on our hands.

'I married young, with 40,000 francs of debts, out of love and calculation, for fear of both marriage and concubinage. My wife had a hundred thousand francs. First we paid off my debts, then we were reduced to pawning her diamonds. She kept the accounts like a good housekeeper, but the word "pawnbroker" terrified her: she inscribed her account book: "Lower Depths". [...]

'You must not worry about pleasing your family! You will never satisfy them. My father went to a play of mine. A man next to him remarked, "How boring this is!" My good father instantly took this as gospel, and the success of the play, the newspaper reports, nothing could wean him away from an opinion which he owed to some incidental fool. Another time, my son spent an evening with some of my enemies, who did not hesitate to run me down. And when he came home, how he sulked over it! I made a note of the faces he pulled, and one day the poor boy will know what I thought of him that evening. My journal is for him, and I wish it never to be published. He can read it after my death. [...]

'You will get there, Renard. I am sure of it, and you will make money, but to do so you'll need to give yourself a good kick up the backside now and then ...'

3 March.

To clean the Augean stables with a toothpick.

7 March.

I read nothing, for fear of coming across something good.

8 March.

Today, went to Daudet's, having arranged to meet there and go on to see Rodin, then Goncourt. Unluckily for me I seem to have displeased Goncourt. Why on earth did I not compliment him blindly on his books, which I haven't read! Ice-cold greeting, the barest civilities [. . .]

Rodin's atelier: a revelation, an enchantment. The *Door of Hell*, and that little thing, no bigger than my hand, called *The Eternal Idol*: a man, vanquished, his arms behind his back, kneels to kiss a woman under the breasts, his lips against her skin, and the woman seems overcome with sadness. I can hardly tear myself away from looking at it. Then an old woman in bronze, a thing of horrible beauty, with her flat breasts, her heavily lined stomach, her still beautiful head. Then various intertwined bodies, knottings of arms – and *Original Sin*, the woman clinging on tightly to Adam, drawing him to her with all her being, and a faun eviscerating a nymph, his hand between her legs, the contrast between the man's calf muscles and the woman's thighs. Lord give me strength to understand these things for what they are!

In the courtyard, blocks of marble waiting to be given life, strangely shaped, as if yearning to live. It is droll: here am I playing the man who has discovered Rodin. [. . .]

Chez Goncourt – a museum from top to bottom. No matter how hard I look, I see nothing. I take in nothing. Goncourt is quite at home in the midst of it all, an old-fashioned specimen of the collector, indifferent to everything that is not his passion. I look at the Daumiers. He holds on to half of a folio that is slipping from my hand: 'They do break, you know.' Then he says:

'If it bores you, you don't have to look at them.'

The house seems curiously insubstantial. The front door of the 'barn' does not close properly, is constantly banging, and all the chinoiserie makes you feel as if you are in one of the more outlandish booths of the Universal Exposition.

9 March.

At Rodin's, as though my eyes were suddenly forced open. Hitherto all sculpture had struck me as rubbishy.

To write as Rodin sculpts.

When I am shown a drawing, I look at it just long enough to think of what I am going to say.

11 March.

Discussion between Raynaud and myself on the subject of Mallarmé. I say: 'It's pointless.' He says: 'It's wonderful.' Model for all literary discussion.

15 March.

With a healthy child we say, unthinkingly: 'I love my child.' But when a child is dying, how to explain how, with its tiny hands, it hooks itself to your heart!

17 March.

Possible scene. The child is dead. Mother and father in tears. The lover takes the woman's hand, claps a hand on the husband's shoulder and says: 'Courage, my friends! We'll make another one.'

23 March.

Balzac is perhaps the only one who earned the right to write badly.

7 April.

Style is the forgetting of all styles.

15 April.

Daudet, in fine form, telling us of the repeated leavetakings of Gauguin, who wants to go to Tahiti in order to find nobody there, but never actually goes. So that in the end even his best friends are telling him: 'You must simply go, my dear fellow, just leave!'

The critic is a botanist. As for me, I am a gardener.

22 April.

Overheard by Schwob's father. At the theatre, a fellow was seated next to a man with a misshapen nose, and suddenly turned to him:

'Excuse me, but I have to say that your nose has been annoying me for the past quarter of an hour.'

Man with the nose: 'Well, it has been annoying me, Monsieur, for twenty-five years.'

24 April.

A man writes a love-letter to a woman, and gets no reply.
He tries to find an explanation for her silence.
He settles on this: 'I should have enclosed return postage.'

27 April.

Yesterday to the Moulin Rouge, Moulin de la Galette. It does no good to discover that you do not exist in the eyes of a desirable woman. A young girl in socks, bare-legged, doing the splits. I would have said yes to being her pimp. I would have said yes to conducting the orchestra, yes to being in charge of the entire spectacle. Ah, the scrofula of vanity . . .

1 May.

What is our imagination, compared to that of the child making a railway track out of asparagus stalks?

7 May.

To take the fleeting idea by the scruff of the neck and flatten its nose against the paper.

My fear of becoming, in the end, a harmless salon version of Flaubert.

9 May.

It is all beautiful. One must write about a pig as about a flower.

Yesterday, the Monet exhibition. Hayricks with blue shadows, fields as gaudy as a chequered handkerchief.

31 July.

Would it never occur to us that a book also has its modesty, and that we should not talk about it to excess?

13 October.

People with good memories possibly lack general ideas.

15 October.

A duel generally has the air of being a stage-rehearsal for a duel.

28 October.

You can catch the tone of the peasantry without resorting to mangled spelling.

30 October.

A solid sentence, as if constructed with shop-sign letters cut out in lead.

2 November.

Astonishing how all literary celebrities gain from being seen in caricature!

Yesterday, collected my first sou from my writing. At such a moment, a sou is worth 50,000 francs.

2 December.

Instead of 1,000 copies, 2,000 copies, etc., it would be more appropriate for publishers to include in our books: first dozen, second dozen, etc.

3 December.

This is all very well, but when do we go to the moon?

4 December.

He was so ugly that when he made faces he became less so.

7 December.

There is only one way of being less of an egoist than others: by admitting to your egotism.

11 December.

I confess, in all humility, my pride.

12 December.

They talk to me a lot about my forthcoming novel, so as not to have to say anything to me after it comes out.

16 December.

It is unfortunate, alas, that our taste improves while our talent stands still.

23 December.

At Schwob's, met André Gide, author of *Les Cahiers d'André Walter*. Schwob introduces me as an insufferably pig-headed individual.

'And if you are not,' says Gide, in a reedy voice, 'you certainly look it.'

He is beardless, has a cold in his nose and throat, a protruding chin, eyes between two rolls of fat. He is besotted with Oscar Wilde, whose photograph is on the mantelpiece: a fleshy gentleman, refined, also beardless, who has recently been discovered.

1892

2 January.

To think we must all die, and that none of us can avoid being born!

4 January.

The motions of the actor who exits on tiptoe while listening out for applause.

5 January.

He was a man embittered by . . . success.

6 January.

I watch the woman whose job is to shuck oysters. She drains off the sea water and adds a little fresh water with a pinch of salt. The diners prefer it that way, she says.

12 January.

Dinner with Schwob:

'Daudet told us the following. He was dining chez Victor Hugo. The poet was presiding, of course, in isolation, at one end of the table, and the guests slowly gravitated towards the young people, Jeanne and Georges. Hugo is by now almost entirely deaf, of course, and no one was speaking to him. He had been practically forgotten, when suddenly, at the end of the meal, the voice of the great man with the shaggy beard was heard – a deep voice, coming from afar: "I have not – been given – any – cake!"' [...]

Schwob also recounted this, of Baudelaire, in a beer tavern, remarking: 'It smells of destruction in here.' – 'Why, no,' he is told, 'an odour of sauerkraut, perhaps, and of warm femininity.' But Baudelaire insists, with violence: 'I tell you, it smells of destruction!'

30 January.

Certain individuals look as if their eyes were on the end of a pole, very far from their brains.

29 February.

The 'ancients' saw character as a whole, a continuity ... We on the other hand see it as discontinuous, with its doldrums and crises, its intervals of goodness and wickedness. The ambition to show things as they are, such as all the great writers had, we have it in spades. But do we get to the truth? Tomorrow or the day after we will falsify it, and so on, until such time as the universe tires of being meaningless.

9 March.

Yesterday, dinner at *La Plume*. Intelligent faces on intelligent men are rare. A concerted ugliness, like the handles of walking sticks. The frightful Verlaine: a dreary Socrates, a soiled Diogenes; part dog, part hyena. Trembling all over, he collapses into a chair that someone carefully places behind him. As for that laughter through the nose – a nose as distinct as an elephant's trunk – through the eyebrows, through the forehead!

When Verlaine enters, a Monsieur who a moment later turns out to be a buffoon, cries out: 'All hail to genius! I don't know him, but all hail to genius!' And claps his hands.

The lawyer for *La Plume* declares: 'The proof of his genius is that he cares nothing for it!'

A few cold meats are brought to Verlaine, who continues brooding.

At the café, he is addressed as 'Maître' and 'cher Maître', but he is distracted, and wants to know what they did with his hat. He looks like a drunken god. All that is left of him is our cult. A ruin of a costume – yellow tie, an overcoat that must be sticking to his bones in several places – propping up a head made of building stone, in the process of demolition. [...]

Verlaine is asked:

'Maître, in what manner have you sinned the most?'

He does not reply, but raises his index finger and points downwards, in a 'speaking' direction.

30 March.

It seems strange that I cannot read two pages of Thackeray without yawning, given that my humour is supposed to resemble his.

6 April.

The new system for writing a novel is not to write a novel.

7 April.

Oscar Wilde next to me at lunch. He has the oddity of being an Englishman. He offers you a cigarette, but selects it himself. He does not walk around a table: he moves the table out of the way. A face worked over by tiny red worms, long cavernous teeth. He is enormous, and carries an enormous cane.

2 May.

And the dog withdrew from the bitch like a red carrot pulled from a jar of lard.

13 May.

In art, never do as others do; in morals, act like everyone else.

1892

14 May.

If only it were enough to stick an exotic stamp on your back to find yourself posted abroad!

2 June.

The peasants say: 'In our land we have everything we need.' But they have no needs.

11 June.

Talent is like money: it is not necessary to have any in order to talk about it.

Already I have made enemies, because I am unable to find talent in all those who tell me I am full of it.

The silver of the moon has lost its value.

13 July.

Shocking! To think that no man has yet committed suicide on my account!

At twenty, one thinks deeply and falsely.

16 July.

Somebody told him that upwardly slanting handwriting was indicative of futurity, so he used it to sign absolutely everything.

25 July.

He is deaf in the left ear: he does not hear on the side of the heart.

The grass is growing out of my penholder.

26 July.

He had a small parakeet, plump as a canary, which sat on his shoulder during meals and ate his hair. Which is why he went bald.

3 August.

Even if inspiration existed, it would be important not to wait for it; and if it came, to drive it away like a dog.

5 August.

I thought you were dead! Oh well, another time.

10 September.

Fear of boredom is the only excuse for working.

19 September.

To be an urchin, playing alone, in the sun, in the square of a little town.

5 October.

The death of others helps us to live.

7 October.

Beneficial for humanity as a whole, catastrophic for each individual.

27 October.

When I came back, the village houses were so small, it was as if I could write the letters of my name on the snow of their roofs with the tip of my finger.

28 October.

The rare and momentary pleasure of feeling that you are improving a little each year.

Lugubrious fanatics. Yesterday we went in pelting rain to the Vélodrome race course, knowing there could not possibly be any races on; we entered, knowing that no one would be there, sat ourselves on a bench in one of the empty stands, and for two hours watched the weeping racetrack, in silence, certain that no competitors would appear; then we left, altogether pleased with ourselves and grinning like lunatics.

4 November.

She has teeth that are worth their weight in gold, literally.

18 November.

Every so often he had to skim off his bubbling thoughts.

21 November.

Rachilde gave me this idea: describe God in the usual terms, granting Him all the omnipotence usually accorded to Him, but varying some of the metaphors, and ending with this: 'Such is God. And there is another Being above Him, concerning whom we know nothing.'

31 December.

The green moons of winter.

1893

3 January.

Docquois tells me:
'What you create are leaves that fall from a tree. Those who do not understand ask themselves where is the tree.'

11 January.

The voluptuousness of telling lies.

When he praises someone, he feels as if he is subtly disparaging himself.

He got into debt, insofar as his resources allowed.

16 January.

'And how is Madame?'
'Doing very well, thank you . . .' But what am I saying! She is dead.

You could see through his beard how ugly he must have been without it.

22 January.

Promise me one thing! If you remarry after I die, promise me that you will make a cuckold of him.

You are worried whether you will be re-read? Then try to be readable in the first place.

First speaker: 'I sell myself, therefore I have talent.'
Second speaker: 'I have talent, therefore I refuse to sell myself.'

25 January.

My pen makes a noise like a goose eating grass.

29 January.

We no longer know how to talk because we no longer know how to listen. There's no point in speaking well: you have to speak quickly, get it out before being interrupted, and there's never enough time. Say whatever you like, however you like: you will always be cut short. Conversation is a game played with shears, in which everyone clips their neighbour's words as soon as they start growing.

1 February. Feast of Peter and Paul.

'Although he already has his imitators, you would not address Jules Renard as "cher Maître". He is too young. Born on 22

February 1864, he was educated at various establishments, the very names of which he has forgotten.

'His ambitions? He has none, he is a literary opportunist.

'His working methods? Each morning he sits at his desk and waits for something to happen. He claims that something always happens.

'Some say: "He is hard-hearted." Others say: "He is a sensitive type who forces himself to seem harsh." Those who claim to know him well say he is "a good sort". Others disagree: "What a grouch! I had no idea he was such a misery-guts."

'Life amuses him in the mornings, and bores him in the evenings.

'As is the case for everyone.

'Charles Cros proclaimed him a poet.'

13 February.

In Geneva. Notice on the Urinals: No Stopping.

I like Maupassant because he seems to be writing for me, not for himself. He rarely goes in for confessions. He does not say, 'Here is my heart,' or, 'The truth comes out of my well and no other.' His books are either entertaining or they are dull. You close them without asking yourself nervously, 'Was that major? Or middling, or minor?' The stormy, excitable aesthetes scorn his name, because it 'returns no echo'.

It is possible that, having read Maupassant in his entirety, you would not wish to do so again.

But those who wish to be re-read will not be read in the first place.

27 March.

Hatred is hardier than friendship; if we could hate our friends we would be of more use to them.

This morning I went to see Papon, who was cutting his lucerne. He stops his work when he sees me coming. He is nearly seventy.

'Well!' he says. 'If I had more to eat, I would get a lot more done.'

He stops scything, bends down to take a bottle of water from his smock, drinks from it and says: 'With a litre of wine now and then, it would take a great deal to kill me off, I can tell you.'

Good for you, Papon!

As for me, because I have a little money and read books and even write them, because I wash and look up at the stars at night, I feel pity for this man who thinks I am above him. No! I am worth neither more nor less than he.

You must love nature and you must love man, in spite of the mud that clings to them both.

1 April.

The business of disentanglement in love-making, when the lips prise themselves away from the skin with difficulty, like stamps on old envelopes. The kisses that leave behind a paste.

26 April.

Capus tells us about a man who was so drunk that he put his boots on the night table and his chamber pot outside the door of his hotel room to be polished.

1 May.

Describe a First Communion: one knee on the pew, the other on the ground, the forgotten rigmarole of words, thoughts exclusively on lunch and the evening to come, demonstrating for all to see that the sacramental 'mystery' means nothing to me. Only the handing around of pious pictures afterwards evokes warm memories.

13 May.

Mendès tells me that Sarcey admits having pronounced the words 'The young man fucked her . . .' to an audience of mothers and daughters, during a lecture in Belgium. Then, correcting himself:

'I should add, Mesdames, that the word did not yet have the meaning that is ascribed to it today.'

19 May.

Young men of twenty tell me:

'You are greater than La Fontaine.'

When I repeat this, I add:

'They are young and know nothing, but are exceptionally intelligent for their age.'

27 May.

One would need another lifetime for art, and then another for music, and so on. In three or four hundred years, one might conceivably complete one's education.

31 May.

If the word 'arse' appears in a sentence, however sublime the sentence, the public will hear only that one word.

14 June.

She asked me to explain shooting stars, and grasped the matter so thoroughly that in the evening, after dark, she took her basket and went out into the fields to look for fallen stars.

15 June.

She says: 'I respect the ideas of others.' In company, however, she advances her opinions, inexorably, like pushing counters in a game of draughts.

8 July.

On the purpose of the tides. The sea moves to and fro, from shore to shore, so as to fill the holes left in the sand by children on the beach.

13 July.

Victor Hugo alone spoke out – other men stammer. They may well have his beard, his broad forehead, his scissor-defeating and indestructible hair (terror of barbers), and the same addiction to playing roles, whether as grandfather or politician. But when I open a book by Hugo – at random, for to choose would be invidious – I am not convinced ... There he seems to be a mountain, a sea, whatever you like – except someone to whom other men might compare themselves.

15 July.

Very pleased with myself for having noticed that, when a woman farts, she always coughs immediately afterwards.

17 July.

Why this air of strangeness which clings to you always, woman I love? I should like to make a deep bow and enquire: 'Who are you?'

5 September.

I am never bored, no matter where I find myself: to be bored is to insult oneself.

Demonstrate that, at bottom, it takes as much intelligence to be a successful grocer as a successful writer.

He tells me that he too loves books, and that recently he even bought an atlas.

Style means the necessary word. The rest matters little.

6 September.

When they broke the news to the politician, 'Your wife is dead,' he replied: 'Is that official?'

We are always happy to discover a family to whom we can moan about our own family.

Possessed of a few sous, I said to myself: 'If I try to earn any more I will be criticized, because I already have some money. But if I content myself with what I already have, I will be told there is no merit in practising my art, for its own sake, given that I have no need to earn a living.' So, after this rather harsh reasoning, I decided to do exactly as I please.

11 September.

Solitude – a place where you can finally blow your nose with enthusiasm.

15 September.

He appeared to be asleep while listening to the womenfolk, but sometimes his long hunter's ears twitched – hunter of stupidities.

19 September.

He preferred a poor theory to a good action.

26 September.

Fantec, who is learning to read, says to his Maman, 'Whisper it to me – very low, just a little.'

30 September.

You look like a hen who says: 'Well, I never! I appear to have laid an egg.'

4 October.

Your sole concern is to be sincere. But don't you find this constant search for sincerity a little false, a little untruthful?

7 October.

In provincial velodromes the starter used to take his own pulse to measure the winning times.

10 October.

Schwob tells a story:
'One day Henri Monnier, invited to a funeral, arriving late, enters the room containing the dead man – by this time deserted

– and putting on his gloves, says to a servant: "So I take it there is no hope?"'

Another anecdote:
'A man following a funeral asks a fellow mourner:
'"Do you know who died?"
'"No, but I think he's the one in the first carriage."'

12 October.

They sprang at each other like two cockerels.
They had seen their fathers gesticulating, raised voices, getting red in the face – in short, having an argument.
When the fathers are gone, the two sons fight until they draw blood, 'to be like Papa'.

14 October.

What is the point of saying 'he has talent', 'he has no talent' . . . Either way there are no *proofs*.

15 October.

Today, when you have a secure job, everyone is cross. And those with mistresses do not acknowledge you in the street.

26 October.

Fantec: 'Now that I'm big, people will think I am a journalist.'

4 November.

In general, nothing so insipid as the conversation of travellers. They have changed places, without changing their ideas.

7 November.

The sun – king of the chrysanthemums.

11 November.

'I would never rescue anyone,' I say. 'I'd be too afraid of finding myself decorated for bravery.'
'As for me,' says Tristan Bernard, 'I once saw a woman under the hooves of a horse. All I could do was scream and take refuge in the nearest urinal.'

12 November.

Bernard addressing a hearse: 'Cabbie, are you free?'

22 November.

One day he married an idea, poor but good, which made him happy for the rest of his life. And they were as penniless on their golden anniversary as on their silver anniversary.

23 November.

Retort of an old woman on her doorstep, at dusk.
'But you cannot see anything, dear lady!'
'I knit to the sound of my fingers.'

1 December.

A new generation is here, like a cuttlefish, spreading its black ink on the blue sea swell.

3 December.

Something out of Jean-Louis Forain. The wife in bed turns her head to watch her husband dressing.
'But these braces aren't my braces!'

7 December.

After all, it is when faced with the subject of death that we feel most bookish.

15 December.

Papa does not look at the person he is addressing: he looks at someone else, and the blood rises and falls in the veins of his forehead like the mercury in a barometer.

1893

18 December.

The way my father's look travels – starting at ground level, then in small steps it reaches my knees, then climbs to my chest – the left eye a little behind the right – and finally meets mine in a union that is embarrassing to us both. His look is steady only when he is angry, and then his pupils stir like a pair of eyeballs at the bottom of a nest.

19 December.

A poet inspired is a poet who writes defective verses.

One-act play. At the end of his life, he confesses something. That one day a young woman, wanting to have a child, threw herself on his mercy. He took her, 'on this very bed'. He has never spoken of it since. In the intervening years he has given his wife glory, fortune, happiness, but always there was this small cloud which came from who knows where, and would never go away. Finally he confesses.

'You are not angry with me?'

'No,' she replies, 'because I too . . .'

And she invents an adultery. Her own cross to bear.

'But I am lying,' she says. 'It is not true. I wanted to show you that you wronged me. So I avenged myself a little. Now it is over. Let us laugh it off.'

But they are so old that they can only smile.

22 December.

Alone, only her avarice remained. She roamed the village, from door to door, trying to sell the rope with which she would subsequently hang herself.

I do not care about knowing many things: I want to know the things I care about.

They were both in the habit of losing, to such an extent that one day when they were playing together, they both lost.

1894

1 January.

Irony is above all a question of wit. Humour is rather a question of the heart, a question of sensibility.

3 January.

As sad as watching someone you love disappear into the fog.

Don't worry! Those of us who fear death always try to die as stylishly as possible.

To live and to be the judge of your life: show me the man who is capable of both.

4 January.

My head is like a poultry-yard. When I call my hen-ideas to give them some corn, it is the duck-ideas, the goose- or turkey-ideas which come running.

There are no friends: there are only moments of friendship.

8 January.

'But after all, you too are something of an artist, in your way, since you are a journalist' – so I am told by M.D., inventor and builder of portable and collapsible houses.

9 January.

What I need is a house in the country – with a telegraph office attached.

10 January.

He used to return visiting cards with the words 'read and approved'.

11 January.

The rain in the gutters makes a sound like someone chewing rubber.

He was a methodical fellow: at lunch he chewed on the right side, at dinner he chewed on the left side.

'Papa,' says Fantec, 'how do watches keep going at night, when they cannot see properly?'

12 January.

People are amazing: they expect us to take an interest in them!

'Fantec, you are too big now to be sleeping with your mother.'
'But I'm not as big as you, Papa!'

Imagine being able to take one's honeymoon alone!

The maid makes a racket with her pans in the kitchen, to drown the noises of Monsieur, who is sitting, embarrassed, in the toilet next door.

15 January.

We get up, in the cold, with a lingering and enigmatic smile on our lips. We have amorous feelings only for the women who appear in our dreams, in our daydreams, who leave behind in our hearts a tiny blue flower which will live for an hour, for the space of a morning after we awaken.

26 January.

Tasted a banana for the first time in my life. Never again, not this side of Purgatory.

To eat well, sleep well, go where one wishes, stay where one pleases, never to complain and, above all, avoid like the plague 'the principal monuments of the town'.

30 January.

What gives me a fever, more than anything, is leafing through a train timetable.

2 February.

The modern man of letters takes copies of everything, so that posterity will have less trouble in assembling his correspondence.

4 February.

He only needed two friends and one enemy – all that was required, in effect, to fight a duel.

When Fantec saw me again after two weeks, he told me I had grown.

20 February.

I like to read as a hen drinks, frequently lifting its head, to let the water trickle down its throat.

22 February.

Thirty years old today, and all around me I feel the waters of melancholy recede.

Thirty years old! Now I'm convinced I shall not escape death.

1894

23 February.

If you are thinking good thoughts about me, better to tell me now rather than later, because, you know, the moment will pass.

26 February.

Axel, by Villiers de l'Isle-Adam, very fine, yes. A cathedral is also very fine, but if one were to put a cathedral on stage . . .

And others admired it only because they were afraid of looking ridiculous.

Finally it was over. We heaved a great sigh of applause.

1 March.

And the grasshoppers we decapitate, without bothering their heads over so trivial a matter, fly out of the window with a flap of their wings!

6 March.

If I were unhappy I would become an anarchist. As it is, I have nothing to complain about.

9 March.

To succeed, well and truly, requires firstly that one gets there oneself, and secondly that others do not.

Since every original comparison necessarily ends up as a banality, make a point of never using them in the first place.

24 March.

Saw Anatole France yesterday. He talks to me about *L'Écornifleur*, which he likes very much, very much. Always a pleasure to have someone praise you for the wrong reasons. I ask him why he called me 'the most sincere of naturalists'.

'By naturalist,' says he, 'I mean someone who loves nature.'

Very well. Moreover, it's of no importance. He will have further occasion to speak of me, and he will get better at it. I tell him:

'My procedure is simple. I am interested in what I write about, and I try to interest others.'

And France, with that screwed-on head of his, turns to Veber and says: 'Very good, what he is saying there. It is very good.'

2 April.

I have a horror of originality.

Happy people have no talent.

5 April.

Some people, Marcel Schwob for example, like foreign writers for the sake of it, out of a taste for foreignness. As for me, I am on my guard, from a preference for my own world. In order for me to find any talent in them, they must have it in spades. I read some Mark Twain, yesterday, for the first time. It seemed very inferior to our own Allais; and what's more, it is too long. I can only bear to be told the cue for a joke. Don't bore us! And then, there's the business of translation: a crime perpetrated by low types who know neither language, and shamelessly set about replacing the one with the other.

6 April.

Vallotton, air of simplicity, gentleness, distinction; flat hair divided by a clear, straight parting; discreet gestures, uncomplicated ideas – and something entirely egotistical in everything he says.

7 April.

To get rid of flies, take off all your clothes and coat yourself head to toe with a glutinous liquid, mixed with a little honey or sprinkled with sugar, then take a slow walk around your bedroom. The flies flock to you, they stick to your skin, you can pick them off at your leisure. As a procedure it may lack elegance, but is infallible.

10 April.

Man is an animal who lifts his head to the skies and sees only the spiders on the ceiling.

She says:
'When he comes back from his mistresses, I wash him, both physically and morally. I am not telling you this to weary you,

Monsieur, but because I watch him falling apart, his talent wasted in the hands of this girl whom I dare not call by her name. I am an honest woman. I am ten years older than he, unfortunately. I have no wish to shackle him. I let him roam; but lately his parents, who know me, who know my worth and that I work hard – for I do work, Monsieur – sent a photograph of him when he was little, saying: "To be forwarded to whom it may concern." Whom it concerns is me, yes, Monsieur! His parents sent me a photograph of G—— as a child.'

12 April.

'In The Hague,' says Courteline, 'people are so clean that when they want to spit they take a train to go and spit in the countryside.'

14 April.

God, whom everyone knows – by name.

A few photographs and a good magnifying glass, and I feel I have travelled sufficiently.

18 April.

He saw as few people as possible, in order to spare himself as far as possible the tedium of funerals.

Take your life seriously – as burlesque.

1894

21 April.

I like rain which lasts all day, and do not feel that I am really in the country unless I am caked with mud.

27 April.

We spend our lives talking about this mystery: our lives.

9 May.

To Fantec:
'Try to get a firmer grip on life than I do, less meanly, and always keep your thoughts at the same height as the trees.'
Dream of big things: it will allow you at least to achieve small things.

11 May.

All the same, I write very nice letters. If only people knew, they would want to know me by my correspondence alone.

My *Journal* must not be simply gossip, as is too often the case with the Goncourts. It must serve to mould my character, correct me, and constantly straighten me out.

15 May.

I complain of my lot, but I have just seen a small child with a wooden leg hitting the ground with all his might, in a rage because he could not keep up with the others.

16 May.

It is not enough to be happy: it is also necessary that others not be happy.

17 May.

My writing is like letters to myself, which I then permit you to read.

Everyone writes their books too soon.

21 May.

A pigeon settles on my window sill, and takes off with a noise like the slap of a shaken napkin.

25 May.

'Why, yes, Fantec, the trees are alive.'
'But not as alive as me,' says he.

26 May.

If you only knew how good I feel when I am quite alone, on what good terms I am with myself!

Ran into Mme Bonnetain yesterday, on the pavement. She is just back from the Sudan. Her pretty face to the wind, nostrils aquiver, she was hand-in-hand with a little yellow girl, exotically dressed, whom she has adopted and brought back from Over There. As for the little white girl, the legitimate daughter, she was walking all by herself in the wake of this couple, her mother and her new sister, for whom the passers-by were all turning their heads.

29 *May*.

Here I am, bald at last. So much the better! What use to me was hair? It was not exactly an ornament, and I was the natural victim of all barbers, an ignoble breed, who exhaled into my face their disdain, or caressed me like a mistress, or patted my cheek like a parish priest.

The thought that I am thirty upsets me. A whole dead life behind me. Ahead, an opaque stretch in which I see nothing. I feel old, and as sad as an old man. My wife looks at me, astonished at my gloom. Little Fantec says to me: 'So you're getting old, Papa?' And, from the world beyond, no one writes to me; no one sends a mark of sympathy or is interested by this lamentable occurrence.

4 *June*.

She has the appearance, old before their time, of certain women who are still young.

I see a date carved on the wall with a knife. I ask her if that was the day of her marriage, or a feast-day, or a birthday. 'No,' she replies. 'It was the day we led the cow to the bull. Exactly six and a half months ago, but her belly does not seem as big as it should be. I felt her again just now.'

For some of the peasants, a grass snake is merely an eel of the hedgerows, and they'll eat it as they would an eel pulled out of the water.

5 June.

Essay on idleness. Describe a day, to show that the brain is like a great flower, which needs to be watered all morning so as to bloom in the evening. And, because in Paris one always goes out in the evening, the brain is never given the chance to reach full maturity. Only in the country can it bloom fully. In the morning, mull over the newspapers, sniff out other people's ideas, take notes with the stub of your pen, see which way the wind is blowing, bring your mind to the point where it needs to express something. In short, keep to this regime, this warm-up routine, and choose words that are light, a language that is neither scientific nor gibberish.

Kidneys, their skins removed, gleaming like chestnuts.

Where would I be happiest? Between two shelves in a cupboard, on a layer of white linen.

14 June.

I would like a study whose window opens onto a farm. I would see the coffee-brown of the pond warming in the sun, the ducks waddling, the geese raising their heads, their hearing as fine as the eye of a needle. Before the cows in the sheds, breathing heavily, I would tell myself: 'It is we men who should take the place of these great beasts. Why do they not with a single toss of their horns eject the cowman who milks them, seated on his stool, emptying their udders two at a time as if he were climbing a rope? And when you try to stroke them they step back. Moreover, the cowman is hardly even aware of his power, his human superiority. I alone get worked up, thinking that I understand, thinking of myself as master. It is because I come back from afar to stand here, in this cowshed. Whereas the cowman is born here.' – And the cap I wear will say, in letters of gilt: 'Nature Interpreter'.

All animals speak, all except the speaking parrot.

The lit petrol of its eyes.

20 June.

Beings, in the form of objects, observe us as we wake up. They were no doubt watching us while we slept. As soon as we open our eyes they stop in their tracks, fearful, and revert to being inanimate.

22 June.

After the condemned man's head is placed under the guillotine, a moment of silence. During which a member of the republican guard breaks from the ranks and gives the hangman an envelope, which the latter opens and says to the condemned man: 'It is your pardon!' – then lets the blade descend.
Thus would the condemned man die in a state of joy.

1 July.

When I open my window, in the morning, it is as if a friend bathed my eyes in cold water.

Small white clouds rise up from the earth as if someone were shearing the wool off its back.

The cockerels, with light or deep voices, throw orders around like young or elderly redskin chiefs.

A far-off train, that will do nicely!

And the voice of a turtle dove, as if a housewife were scraping the remains of a crème brûlée from a casserole with a wooden spoon – or rather, as if one kept coming in and going out to test the hinges of a door.

And a hen is cackling as if she were tapping her freshly laid egg on an anvil, with quick little taps.

And a fly buzzes past, just like the sound that runs along a telegraph wire.

And the three long strokes of a bell, followed by three long strokes, followed by a chime, brisk and light.

And the voices of the ducks, like pebbles that skim along the ice of the canals in winter.

And the voices of men have yet to be heard.

And their first words are these: 'Close the window! Go back to bed!'

4 July.

His advice was: read the news in brief, each day, so as to comprehend your own good fortune.

9 July.

The best interviewer was the one who said I have the eye of an eagle and the mane of a lion.

When her dog died she said to her husband:
'I would like it so much if you were to wear a little crape in your hat, just two fingers, a tiny amount.'

17 July.

As for imagination, I have not a scrap of it. I'd be incapable of making up even a magazine story.

The moon on a lightning rod, like a clown who spins a hat on the end of a stick.

I quote the example of Pascal who fought off his headaches by solving problems in geometry.
'In my case,' says Tristan Bernard, 'I fend off geometry by pretending to have headaches.'

18 July.

Do not say that what I write is not true – for everything is true; say rather that I tell it badly.

22 July.

Jules Renard, a pocket Maupassant.

23 July.

Schwob's explanation, on the impossibility of starting up a morning newspaper in Nantes: because the pavements are so narrow that people cannot read while walking to work.

25 July.

Whatever happens, I shall have *pulled off* six years of happiness, since I got married, in 1888.

26 July.

Baïe and Fantec do not want to be given the same toys, because they prefer to be jealous of each other and cry and squabble.

I could not stop myself saying to the news vendor:
'You see that little book? – I wrote it.'
'Really?' says she. 'I've yet to sell a single copy.'

To Fantec: 'Death, it's like that little bird which you never saw again.'

31 July.

Arromanches.
The great clock was lying on the ground, as if time had been put in a coffin.

23 August.

A little beggar comes prowling around us. I am told he pretends to be an imbecile but has all his wits about him. We tell him: 'Say your prayers and you'll be given a sou.' He hesitates, sticks a finger in his mouth, pulls out an enormous plug of tobacco which he throws on the ground, then kneels and says his prayer, intoning: 'Lord, I offer up my heart.' Then gets to his feet, after making a hurried sign of the cross, picks up his tobacco plug and waits for his money. He is both amusing and revolting.

21 September.

Poil de Carotte is a poor thing, unfinished, ill-written, because it only came to me in gusts.

We are never happy: our happiness is merely the silence of our unhappiness.

27 September.

Poil de Carotte could as well be shorter or longer. *Poil de Carotte* is a state of mind.

1 October.

To do for my village what Sainte-Beuve did for Chateaubriand and his time. Tell everything through notes, small dramas or mute tableaux – everything, up to the terrors of the night. Dig right down, hold up the plant of reality along with its roots.

Memory, bring me my country, put it here, on the table. The difficulty is that before you can recall a place you must enter it, sink your feet into its mud.

19 October.

Aim all my literary firepower at my village. Bring to bear on this subject all that I value most in literary terms.

23 October.

To go for a walk on the day your book appears, casting side glances at the stacks of copies, as though the sales assistant were watching you; then to reckon that any bookseller who has not put it in the window (or who has merely not received any copies yet) is your mortal enemy . . . And generally to behave like someone who is being flayed alive. Books are nowadays so many cakes of soap! At Flammarion's, I used to hear the clerk calling out: 'One *Poil*! Two *Poil*! Three *Poil*!'

It would seem that if you are on good terms with Achille, the Calmann-Lévy bookseller, Boulevard des Italiens, you have an assured sale of 100 copies. But Achille is not an easy proposition. He has his favourites. The paltry offer of an author's copy with a handsome dedication may not suffice. He has even been known to show regular customers the door. An eccentric, who no doubt has a healthy contempt for all men of letters.

1894

3 November.

I am a clock whose pendulum travels unceasingly between pride and abjection. With a firm footing, however. I keep my balance and stay upright.

6 November.

Yesterday, at the Théâtre de l'Œuvre, *'Tis Pity She's a Whore*, by John Ford, translation by Maeterlinck. Conversation by Marcel Schwob. Despite which, a pervasive odour of barbarity. This brother and sister talk like lovers. Ideally, incest would be the tranquil culmination of two young lives. If we calmly accepted incest the world could be remade from scratch.

12 November.

What I would like is to be a village schoolmaster, writing articles for the local newspaper, dispensing rural wisdom, safely out of sight of the sceptics.

26 November.

Lautrec: a tiny blacksmith behind a pince-nez. Wearing a little sack with two compartments for his poor withered legs. Thick lips, and hands like the hands he draws, with bony, wide-apart fingers, thumbs bent into semicircles. He often brings small men into his conversation with an air of saying: 'A good thing I'm not *that* small!' [...]

He has his own room in an 'establishment', is on good terms

with all the girls, who have a delicacy and refinement unknown to honest women, and who pose admirably. He also owns a former convent, so he moves between convent and 'home'.

At first his smallness is painful to see; but then he is so alive, and so agreeable, with a kind of grunt that punctuates his sentences and swells his lips, as the wind puffs the draught-excluder of a door. [. . .]

Always the same little grunt, and the desire to tell you things that are 'so stupid that they are brilliant'.

And bubbles of saliva take refuge in his moustache.

She is one of these dainty little women who prefer to love than to make love.

9 December.

Yesterday, Lautrec's atelier with Tristan Bernard. From the street and the pouring rain we enter a stifling workshop. In his shirtsleeves, trousers falling down, wearing a flour merchant's hat, tiny Lautrec opens the door. Straight away I notice, on a sofa towards the rear of the atelier, two naked women: one showing her bust, the other her backside. Bernard walks straight up to them and shakes their hands, saying: 'Good day, young ladies!' I am in a panic of embarrassment and haven't the courage to look openly at the two models. I cast about for a place to put my hat, my coat, my leaking umbrella.

'Don't let us keep you from working,' says Bernard.

'We are done,' says Lautrec. 'You may get dressed, ladies.'

He fetches a ten-franc piece and places it on the table. They get dressed, partly behind the canvases, and from time to time

I risk a glance, without seeing anything properly; I seem to feel their defiant looks upon my lowered eyes. At last, they leave. I have glimpsed olive-skinned buttocks, pendulous breasts, red hair, yellow fur.

Lautrec shows us studies he has made in various 'establishments', his apprentice work. Right from the start it was bold and defiant. He strikes me as more interested in art than anything else. I am not sure if what he produces is good, but I know that he seeks out what is uncommon, that he is an artist. This little man who calls his walking stick 'my little cane', who undoubtedly suffers on account of being short, has the sensibility of a man of talent, if nothing else.

12 December.

I was born for success in journalism, for everyday renown, for the literature of abundance. Reading great writers changed all that. Whence proceeds all my misfortune.

18 December.

What is this new religion of humanity? Are we any better today than we were yesterday? Or have they just discovered the thousandth new subject for a novel: 'Humanity'. Until now humanity interested nobody. One might say that as a subject it did not exist, and no writer bothered with it. What did our fathers talk about, I wonder.

1895

15 January.

At the zoo.

Seals sticking their elbows out awkwardly, like the natives of the Auvergne when they go out into the world. Their little pursed ears, pink faces planted with black stumps of teeth.

Tiny parakeets, like singing tie-pins.

The hamadryas baboons, dressed for a coming-out ball, their way of peeling raw potatoes, their sudden and prolonged howling, mouths wide open.

1 February.

How monotonous snow would be, had God not created crows.

4 February.

Grass. I want to try putting a village into a book, and to put it in whole, from the mayor to the pig inclusive. And they will understand the beauty of the title who have ever heard a peasant say: 'The grass is growing,' or 'Good weather for grass,' or 'There's no grass left.'

8 February.

The snow swirls like a Loie Fuller dancer.

13 February.

Yes, the story I am writing exists, faultlessly written, floating about somewhere in the atmosphere. All I have to do is find it – and copy it out.

18 February.

Publishers are such nice people, when they are not your publisher.

19 February.

Toulouse-Lautrec. The more you see of him, the taller he gets. He ends by being taller than average.

24 February.

I only like talking with people taller than me, whose mouths are level with my head, so their breath rises above me.

25 February.

To the peasants who ask him if this part of Paris is far from that part, Papa replies. 'Bah! there is just a river to cross.'

2 March.

Last night, banquet for Edmond de Goncourt. You may be excused for non-attendance, by sending a telegram in advance. Saving: 12 francs. What is more, the telegram will be read out over dessert, so you have thereby called attention to yourself...
[...]

'We don't see you often enough,' Goncourt tells me.

'Mon cher Maître, I stay away purely out of discretion.'

'Well it's *silly* of you!'

'Now there is a word I like.'

He is handsome, our cher Maître. He is moved, and when you shake his hand, it feels soft and pneumatic, as though filled with the water of his emotion.

On the table in front of him, a magnificent gateau, rather like a pastry-cook's scale model of the Académie Goncourt.

What! Is that the great Clemenceau, the gentleman with one hand in his pocket, talking in a clipped voice, trading his faded formulas? Was this same scalpel not used to sever the main artery of a mammoth? Lord, how remote these people are from mere mortals! 'The honest working man ... a social Republic ...' Come, come, Monsieur, you are among men of letters, do you mistake us for voters? Do you not sense our disappointment, even our scorn? Some of your friends say you make it up as you go along ...

And over here is Zola, forever talking shop. Ah! the old logger, still logging away. And here at last is Daudet, who remains seated, reading aloud to Goncourt his homework on the subject of friendship. He even looks like a schoolboy at his table, bent over his tremulous sheet of paper, under the stern eye of the master.

And yet I declare that our hearts went out to them when, in the midst of bravos and applause, Goncourt and Daudet pressed each other's hands under the table.

7 March.

The certainty of not being alone, even in a cemetery, consoles us.

16 March.

Yesterday, went for the first time in my life to the Opéra.

19 March.

At Claudel's, spectral supper and aftermath. His sister says:
'You frighten me, Monsieur Renard. You will put me in one of your books and make fun of me.'
Her powdered visage is inanimate except for the eyes and mouth. At times it seems entirely lifeless. She hates music, says very loudly what she thinks, while her brother rages silently, his nose in his plate, and you sense his hands tightening with rage and his legs trembling under the table.

13 April.

In the Oscar Wilde affair, what is even more comical than the indignation of the whole of England, is the dumb-show of outrage on the part of certain Frenchmen with whom we are all too well acquainted.

8 May.

Mallarmé. His conversation is so clear that, after reading him, his talk seems banal by comparison. He talks about Baudelaire, about what I am doing. Despite myself, I remain ice-cold. Unable to manage a pleasant word. If at least he were as hairy as his faun I could stroke him.

At the zoo. The shirt-button eyes of the pink flamingoes.
A bison, sculpted in stone, except for the moving jaws.
A black swan with red bill, like an alcoholic priest.
The ibex as solemn as a reaper coming home from the fields, a two-edged sickle on his shoulder.

30 May.

Prudence is merely a euphemism for fear.

29 June.

I know why I detest Sundays: it is the sight of other people, having nothing to do, allowing themselves to be as idle as myself.

The storm is playing *boules* behind the mountain. After each clap of thunder it rains even harder, like tears after an exchange of strong words.

6 July.

The poet Titulopanpé had written a poem on butterflies. He was not happy with the result. He found the flight of his butterflies too heavy. He tore up his poem and threw the pieces of paper into the lake. But they did not fall into the water. Carried off by the breeze, they shimmered in flight. And the poet Titulopanpé followed them with his eyes, feeling moved and happy to have written a poem which was better than he knew.

27 August.

When others tire me, it is because I am tired of myself.

28 August.

I am often dissatisfied with what I have written. I am never dissatisfied with what I am writing, otherwise I would not be writing it.

30 August.

The concierge's little daughter, who has been struck blind, begins to make very good use of her other faculties: she comes and goes, even venturing out onto the pavement: but when she hears other children playing in the street, she goes back inside and cries.

2 September.

My brain is stuffed with literature and swollen like a goose's liver.

9 September.

Poil de Carotte is ahead of me at every moment. We share a life, and I only hope that I die before he does.

19 September.

Histoires Naturelles. Buffon described animals in such a way as to please humans. Whereas I want to please the animals themselves. I would like my book, if they could read it, to make them smile.

He likes to travel. What bores him is changing places.

22 September.

Paradise does not exist, but we must nevertheless strive to be worthy of its existence.

Impossible to see into the depths of my heart: the candle goes out down there, for want of fresh air.

I already feel old, incapable of great things. If my life is prolonged for another twenty years, what shall I do with them?

30 September.

I want my ear to be a shell that holds all the sounds of nature.

And if a leaf which seemed sheltered suddenly begins to shake, to become delirious (yes! it is a delirium), while its neighbours remain calm, is there not a mystery in this?

2 October.

Don't delude yourself! Born twenty years earlier, you'd have been a Naturalist like the rest of them.

3 October.

As for my lyre, I lit the gas and set fire to it.

9 October.

My brother Maurice tells me: 'Papa and I sit together on the wall. He waits for me to talk, I wait for him to talk. And this goes on until we go to bed.' He can no longer hunt. He has a pain in his left arm. When a partridge starts up, or a hare bolts, he cannot lift his arm. It is as though someone were putting a hand on his shoulder, to stop any more killing, saying: 'Enough!'

21 October.

The crow: always on its way back from a funeral. A magpie in half-mourning.

25 October.

Papa as mayor.

'The town drummer receives twenty-five francs a year.'

'Which is not enough to keep his drum in condition,' I say.

'In the first place, the drum does not belong to him. It belongs to the commune. Moreover, I seldom ask him to drum. The only drumming he does is at election time. If I keep him occupied for one hour a year, that is an hour well paid. Besides, it is an honour. The drum rightfully belongs to the local ranger, whom my predecessor, for whatever reason, removed from his post. This drummer is an eccentric. He showed up the other day to saw my woodpile carrying a serrated knife.'

He continues:

'Every commune now has free medical assistance; and we give bread to the poor. There are unfortunates in Chitry, but not a single beggar. Beggars are not permitted to leave their commune. With a lump of bread and a few nuts, you can make do. There were two that came to see me from Saint-Révérien, a blind man led by a young woman.

'"But can your wife not work," I said to him, "instead of leading you about like that all day long?"

'"Well, Monsieur le maire, but that would bring in less money."

'I gave them a sou anyway, telling them not to come back, or I would have them locked up. I watched them go off along the old road. I could hear them laughing. They were making fun of me.'

27 October.

Papa never sends a wire in advance to say he is coming, because in this life you know when you leave, but not when you will arrive. So he appears unexpectedly, from twenty miles away, with a partridge in his pocket.

He speaks so slowly that he only ever replies to your last question but one.

29 October.

The greatest error of the law is to assume that the defendant always acts from rational motives.

31 October.

Jules Renard, Mayor of Chaumot – that will look well on the covers of my books . . .

2 November.

Papa. The swollen veins of his temples. The moles are at work, ravaging him beneath the skin.

5 November.

There is no unity; there is only discontinuity.

15 November.

The rabbit has the human gesture of a man combing his beard.

16 November.

Add a few letters to 'Paris' and you get 'Paradise'.

17 November.

Yesterday, in the grounds of Bellevue, on a broad avenue where the trees were losing their leaves and dying like mute poets, a madwoman.

We were in a carriage. She ran behind us and spoke hurriedly:

'Do you know my family? They are from Normandy. You would like them so much if you knew them.'

She was well-dressed, still young, air of refinement.

A nun walked beside her, and from time to time castigated her:

'Now leave these gentlemen in peace! Come along, quickly!'

The nun let her wander off for a hundred paces. Then called her back sharply. The madwoman no longer paying any attention, who owes it to her wealth that she does not have to go begging in the ditches.

27 November.

Keep their interest! Keep their interest! Art is no excuse for boring people.

2 December.

Modesty suits great men. What is hard is to be modest when one is a nobody.

What use is good fortune if there is no joy!

6 December.

I am happy to sign the petition for Oscar Wilde, on condition that he give his word of honour to desist from . . . writing.

I have known happiness, but that is not what has made me happiest.

9 December.

As soon as you stop being serious with a friend, a rupture is close at hand. I know the signs, having gone through friends by the dozen.

13 December.

The commonplace and petty cowardice of siding with others against a friend.

If you are acquainted with Life, give me her address.

26 December.

Descaves tries to persuade me that I need fifty *Histoires Naturelles* to make a volume. It isn't his opinion alone: others share it, etc. etc. Lautrec suggests that he might illustrate eight of them and we could sell a hundred copies at twenty-five francs a piece, sharing the profits.

Lautrec likes bars, no doubt on account of the stools, on which he can perch, for then he is nearly as tall as the rest of us.

Sarah Bernhardt. I am searching for a phrase that will sum up my impressions of her. I find only this: 'very nice'. I had no desire to meet her in the flesh. Now I have destroyed the ridiculous and embarrassing idol I had made of her. What remains is a woman whom I had believed slim but who is plump, whom I believed ugly but who is pretty, yes, as pretty as a child's smile.

When Rostand said, 'May I present Jules Renard,' she rose at once from her dressing table and said in a tone that was joyous, childlike, charming:

'Oh, how happy I am! He is just as I thought he would be – isn't that so, Rostand? Monsieur, I am one of your admirers.'

'Madame, it is the greatest amazement of my life to learn that you might admire the works (I said it: *the works*) of Jules Renard.'

'Why?' said she. 'Did you think I was too stupid?'

'There! Now I have said something stupid.'

'Not at all!'

And she puts some rouge on her lips.

Later, on the stairs, I found this to say: 'No, Madame, I took you for a woman of genius, with all the pressures that this entails.' Which was probably even more stupid.

'Just feel how cold I am,' she says, brushing Rostand's cheek with her hand. She calls him 'my poet', 'my author'.

'It's true. You are frozen,' says Rostand.

And I can find no words! Not a hope of appearing brilliant. I am strongly moved, am overcome, and how I wish I were a man of the world.

'What are you doing at the moment, Renard?'

'Madame, I have just done something very fine: I have been listening to you.'

'Yes, you are a darling. But what are you writing?'

'Oh, nothing much. Small things, natural histories of the animals. Less handsome than this one,' I say, pointing to her dog, a superb creature she calls Djemm, I believe.

And my poor man's voice is lost in the dog's fur.

1896

1 January.

Wanting this to be an exceptional year, I start by getting up late, eating too much for lunch, and fall asleep in an armchair until three in the afternoon.

2 January.

Chez Sarah Bernhardt. She is reclining, near a monumental fireplace, on the pelt of a polar bear. Because in her house you do not sit down, you recline. She says to me: 'Put yourself there, Renard.' There? Where is there? Between her and Mme Rostand, a large cushion. Not daring to sit on it, I kneel at Mme Rostand's feet, and my feet stick out, stick way out, as in a confessional.

The assembled company is terrified of the number thirteen. Maurice Bernhardt is there, with his pregnant young wife. Sarah takes my arm to go into the dining-room. Which is enough to make me forget to lift the door-curtain. I release her as soon as we reach the first plate, but it is way over on the other side that we are headed, towards that big chair with the canopy. I sit at her right, and do not expect to do much eating. Sarah drinks from a golden cup. I seem to be incapable of speech, nor of asking for my napkin, which a footman has taken away; so I eat meat with my fruit fork. A moment later I catch myself neatly placing my sucked asparagus stems across my knife-rest. Next I am confounded by a certain glass platter: it is for the salad. Fortunately, on Sarah's left side there is one of those ubiquitous society doctors one always finds in novels, on the stage, and in real life. He is explaining to Sarah why it is that last night she heard twenty-one knocks, and why her dog barked twenty-one times.

Next there is the reading of palms. I am under the influence of the moon, it seems. I simply must nurture the moon, talk about the moon, succumb to the moon's phases. It is true that I do talk a lot about the moon, but I seldom look at it. Close inspection reveals that my thumb displays more will to power than good sense. Which is true enough. Rostand is the opposite. Sarah takes and retakes my hand, which is white and plump, as far as that goes, but let down by poorly kept fingernails. Never have I seen them as I see them tonight, neither shapely nor clean. [. . .]

'I had scarcely read a line of yours for the first time,' says Sarah, 'when I thought: this man simply has to be ginger. Though redheads are usually mean-spirited. Besides, you are rather on the blond side.'

'I was indeed a redhead, once, downright ginger and frankly vicious, Madame, but as goodness took hold, and the faculty of Reason, my hair went blond.'

And more idiocies of this sort. [. . .]

In walks a lion, one of the five 'pumas' of Sarah Bernhardt. He is led on a chain, and goes around sniffing various skins and at their owners. He has a dreadful extension of haunch, of claws, and Haraucourt does well to close his eyes when the 'puma' shows an inclination to caress his ruffed shirt front. At last, more or less to everyone's relief, the lion is led away.

Next come two enormous dogs with pink pug noses: either of whom might happily consume a child for its supper. They roll around on the floor, gentle, well-behaved, and fairly soon our clothes are covered with little white hairs.

A bottle of champagne is overturned while it is being opened by a footman. The cork goes off, and Sarah, stretched out on her bearskin, receives the contents full in the face. For a moment, I thought it was all part of the entertainment.

At the end of the evening I could not find my hat, because it was already on my head, so I calmly walked off with someone else's hat in my hand.

8 January.

The giant kangaroo. As if he broke his own legs, so as to walk on all fours, but even now his arms are still too short.

9 January.

Funeral of Verlaine. As a certain academician once said, funerals are enlivening. They give me back my vitality. [...]

Verlaine had gone to Holland to lecture. The best room in the hotel had been reserved for him. He summoned the manager:

'I want another room.'

'Maître, this is our best room.'

'Precisely. As I said: I want another one.'

He had brought a suitcase which contained nothing but a dictionary.

1896

18 January.

I love Rostand, and I am happy to force others (Bernard, Boulenger) to love Rostand too. He is my 'far-away prince', as well as a little brother whose suffering face pains me. I am constantly afraid of news of his death, of having him slip from my grasp. He is delicate and gentle, without any meanness. He is perhaps very unhappy. He avoids faces he does not know, and is happy to know that he is loved. Yes, it may be so: that despite his luxuries, his lovely wife, his burgeoning fame – he is unhappy. His death would cause me pain, very great pain.

Oh, come on! Let me be a little ridiculous, just for once.

Taking notes is the literary equivalent of practising scales.

25 January.

First admission: I do not always understand Shakespeare. Second admission: I do not always like Shakespeare. Third admission: I do always feel bored by Shakespeare.

31 January.

A style as fat and slippery and treacherous as Parisian cobbles on a foggy day.

3 February.

'Lautrec is so small,' says Mme T. Bernard, 'that he gives me vertigo.'

The snow lingers, here and there, as traces of soap sometimes lurk in the ears.

7 *February*.

Rostand: He has a fine study, but he does no work there. He works in a bedroom, on a rickety little table. After his *Romanesques* was staged he treated himself to a handsome bathroom, with a bidet beside the bath. When his sister-in-law enters she addresses him as 'cher Maître'.

He isolates himself, more and more. He finds us all false, untrue, spiteful, rapacious . . .

He says he is always able to find talent in those he detests, or despises.

'The modest half-mourning of her white polka-dot coat,' he remarks of the guinea-fowl. [. . .]

'So? And what do you have for me?'

That is how he greets me this evening, after keeping me waiting.

'You have become insufferable!' I tell him. 'I shall remain young, and leave you to your chosen decrepitude. Good day!'

'Agreed – let's put an end to this farce!'

His eyes are small and narrowed. He curls his moustache. He is pale.

'Rostand, there are only a very few ties left to connect us, a few trifles, and now I am severing them.'

'Go ahead!'

As I am closing the door, I hear:

'What a disgusting nuisance, really!'

I turn around. I say *au revoir*, and add that the weather outside is lovely.

'You'd better go and enjoy it', says he.

I am shaking with anger, and his lips are white. Perhaps we are both experiencing a savage joy to be turning our backs on each other.

One friend the less – what a relief!

10 February.

Salomé, by Oscar Wilde. Impressive, but you'd need to cut off, here and there, some of the many heads of Jokanaan. There are too many of them, too many! And so much unnecessary shouting, and such fake finery!

At the zoo. I notice a cage, inside which a small animal is constantly coming and going, with a dark tenacity. It is not displeasing: rather, it is comical. I think I know what it is, as a specimen, but I hesitate, and then I run into the keeper.

'Monsieur, what might this new arrival be,' I ask, 'whose cage has no label?'

'That one? Wait a moment!' he replies. 'I cannot remember its name. There were two of them, you know, running through the grass, a week ago, chasing after one another. What the devil is it, it's on the tip of my tongue.'

He thinks. We think together.

'Aha!' he says suddenly. 'I have it! Now I remember. Well, Monsieur, I'm afraid it's . . . a small dog.'

13 February.

'We painters have a saying,' says Jean Veber, 'that no model can distract us. As for me, the model distracts my attention, quite a bit, and I find it very difficult.'

As for me, I am so embarrassed that I don't even say hello to the model, and can only look at her furtively; but I feel her gaze resting upon me.

I am no bourgeois, but I experience some of the bourgeois virtues.

20 February.

Dinner chez Alphonse Allais. A bohemian who spent his youth and not a few of his mature years in cafés and furnished rooms, here he is settled into an apartment worth 3,500 francs. Bathroom. Continuous hot water. Visitors need only turn on the tap to scald themselves. There is a cook, and a butler called Gaëtan, who brings letters on a salver and says timidly, 'Madame is served.'

'Do you not want to giggle when you say that?' Allais asks him.

He has furniture which he brought back from England, elegant and refined, 'admirably designed', says Gandillot, who seats himself in a chair which immediately lets out an alarming groan. While waiting for the chandeliers to arrive, electric bulbs shine inside mistletoe. Mistletoe on all floors.

I too will one day have an expensive apartment, for which I shall pay a lot more than 3,500 francs! Alas no. I would prefer a road-mender's cabin.

And everything comes from England: glasses, salt cellars . . . even the soup, for it is cold, and the steak, for it is over-cooked.

There is also some antique vinegar which has gone off and turned into a jolly decent little wine.

1 March.

There is no use in dying: you have to die when you are properly cooked.

12 March.

'There's something of the priest about you, Renard. You can never forget your first communion. You are on the side of morality, chastity, duty.'

'That is correct. I am fed up with our literature, which is saucy doggerel about nothing except cuckolds.'

1 April.

When he drinks with a couple, he always pays the bill, so that people will think he is the lover.

8 April.

You must not laugh at the external aspect of things, you must enter into their spirit. One must laugh from the centre of things. In other words, I do not laugh at politics *per se*, because there may be some good in it, of which I am ignorant. But I laugh at the politicians I know, at first hand, and at the politics they practise in front of my eyes. Rather than frivolity, laughter must be serious and informed, and philosophically awake! You have a right to cry with laughter only when you have already wept. The ridiculous belongs to the moment, and nothing is entirely or permanently ridiculous.

You must laugh only at what you could love in other circumstances. The commonplace does not provoke laughter. Before mocking great men you must know how to love them with all your heart.

Laughter is impregnable because it laughs at itself, but it dies by itself in solemn and thoughtful company.

[Ernest] Renan said: 'The mockers will never rule.' Which is true, they laugh at the very idea of ruling.

11 April.

The sky is a continuation of the slate roof.

17 April.

The progress of an intellectual: (1) stupefaction; (2) irony; (3) enthusiasm.

What is the eye doing there, behind its lid ...

21 April.

If I had talent, I would be imitated. If I were imitated, I would become fashionable. If I were fashionable, I would soon go out of fashion. Better therefore to be talentless.

1896

26 May.

Chaumot. *La Gloriette*. He has bought a sprayer for his vines. It looks not unlike the contraption the liquorice-water vendors carry on their backs. To check that it was working properly, he examined the nozzle, turned on the tap, and received a jet of vitriol in both eyes. He ran like a madman to the gutter, washed his eyes with muddy water, since when his eyes weep incessantly, and are as red as coral rings. But the sprayer is an improvement. Oh yes, a great improvement.

Life is short, and yet how long, from cradle to grave!

June.

I thought I was getting old. I saw Raymond yesterday. I used to play with him. What a wreck! Thin, bent double, hands encrusted, teeth black, eyes lifeless. Raymond is old.

An obvious enough remark: it wears you out, working from five in the morning to seven at night, with no nice cuts of meat. It is pleasant, a daily intake of salad and fresh soft cheese. That and modern life, and fresh country air, will kill a man in thirty years.

As for me, I check in the mirror every week for more white hairs.

13 June.

At the onset of winter, it is customary here for the ranger and a local mason to do a tour of inspection of the houses in the village. They examine the chimneys, test the ovens, and have a drop of wine. By the tenth house, they are drunk. Each of them gets three francs a day, and the job lasts three days.

This year, when Papon came to tell the mayor that he was about to start his tour of inspection, my father – who already had to sack him last year – abolished the custom, which has no basis in law. He told Papon:

'If it pays you nine francs, I'll pay you eighteen francs to keep you in order.'

Despite having to forgo the drops of wine, Papon replied: 'As you wish, Monsieur le maire. It makes no difference to me.'

But then Papa forgot to give him the eighteen francs.

July.

It is deceitful to try to be kind. You must be born kind, or else have no truck with kindness.

After reading a lecture by professor Carl Vogt on the usefulness of the mole, I killed one with a single rifle blast. I had watched it raising its mound of fresh earth: twice I destroyed the mound. It made another. So I unblocked its hole. It came up for some air. I killed it like a god, with my own thunderbolt, steeling myself a little, just to see how it was done. For the mole it must have been like a thunderclap, were it to come crashing directly overhead. I killed it as though I were a god! It was in the middle of the path, minding its own business. Not touching my heads of salad, about which I care so little. But I killed it anyway. Why? Meanwhile the cat has just made its mess in my armchair, and I say nothing.

9 July.

A ginger style. If literature has different colours, I imagine mine would be ginger.

Clouds, clouds, where are you running off to? It is so pleasant here!

14 July.

I realize with amazement that I am not cut out for country life.

I am made only to listen to the earth and watch it breathe.

If you brought news of the death of my little girl, whom I love so much, and if there was something vivid in the way you expressed yourself, I would not hear it without being charmed.

18 July.

With all due respect for the Sermon on the Mount, if you thirst for righteousness you will thirst forever.
Incapable of 'sustained effort', I read a little here and there, and write a little here and there. And I firmly believe this is the destiny of the true artist.
As though he had read Fénelon on *L'Éducation des Filles*, Papa was always setting Jesus Christ before us as an example: 'Until He was thirty, Christ worked as a carpenter.' True enough, but in the end tiresome.

'One of these days,' says Papa, 'I must sit down and write out a few lines for my will.' Two lines, to be precise: 'I want a civil burial. Do with my corpse as you please.'

August.

We always confound the man and the artist, merely because chance has brought them together in the same body. La Fontaine wrote immoral letters to his womenfolk, which does not prevent us from admiring him. It is quite simple: Verlaine had the genius of a god, and the soul of a pig. Those who were close to him must have suffered. It was their own fault! – they made the mistake of being there.

September.

The river. Reeds, the upright bayonets of drowned regiments.

Pastorals. The perfectly tranquil manner in which animals do battle. Two rams butt each other in the head furiously, then revert to grazing, then again rush at each other passionlessly.

Same thing observed with cockerels.

'Dear God!' cried Mme Lepic. 'What have I done to be so unhappy! Oh, my poor Poil de Carotte, if I ever tormented you, I beg your forgiveness!'

She spouts tears like the roof gutters.

Then suddenly, dry-eyed: 'Ah, if my poor leg did not give me so much trouble I would run away from here. I would eke out a living washing the dishes in a rich house.'

There is nothing harder to confront squarely than the face of a mother you do not love, who inspires nothing but pity.

18 October.

Mme Lepic used to change her chemise in front of me. To tie the laces over her breasts, she would lift her arms and neck. Again, as she warmed herself by the fire, she would tuck her dress up above her knees. I would be compelled to see her thigh; yawning, or with her head nestling in her hands, she would rock to and fro on her chair. My mother, of whom I cannot speak without terror, used to set my blood on fire.

The fire has remained in my veins. In the daytime it sleeps, but at night it awakens and I have fearful dreams. In the presence of M. Lepic, who reads his newspaper and does not even glance in our direction, I take my mother, who is offering herself to me, and I re-enter that womb from whence I came. My head disappears into her mouth. The pleasure is infernal. What an agony of awakening there will be tomorrow, and how black I shall feel all day! Immediately afterwards we are enemies again. Now I am the stronger. With those same arms that passionately embraced her, I throw her to the ground, I crush her; I trample her underfoot, I grind her face into the kitchen tiles.

My father, meanwhile, continues reading his newspaper, quite unconcerned.

If I knew in advance that tonight I would have the same dream, I swear I would flee the house instead of going to bed. I would walk until dawn, and would not drop with exhaustion, because fear would keep me on my feet, sweating and running.

Farce and tragedy combined: my wife and children call me Poil de Carotte.

21 October.

'It ought to be enough,' he told her, 'that in reality I am faithful to you – so allow me at least to keep up the appearance of being an unfaithful husband.'

23 October.

As we are about to leave, Maman gives a box to Marinette. It contains a chicken, butter, fruit. She adds:

'Be sure to send me back the box! Take good care of it!'

And she sings the praises of her box.

She knows very well that Marinette will return it to her filled with coffee and good things from Paris.

27 October.

While talking, he directs a quantity of spittle in my direction, almost a gob of spit. He does not wipe it off. Nor do I wipe it off. I avenge myself by not wiping it off, and he has to keep talking, his eye drawn unavoidably to the spittle; there is something between us, after all.

28 October.

My *psyche*. – I feel that I am becoming more and more of an artist, and less and less intelligent. Some things that I understood, I no longer understand, and each moment something new troubles me.

1 November.

My *Psyché*. – Enough of being described as a keen observer! Nothing bores me as much as observation. I watch the world timidly. Each new piece of information alarms me. If I am told, 'Turn right, and you will encounter a perfect specimen of humanity,' I will keep going regardless. I submit to whatever I see, but I do not seek it out.

7 November.

Admirers. The provincial critic who discovers us and instantly becomes an expert. He writes a preliminary study in his local paper. We thank him politely: 'Ah, if only Paris had a few critics with your discrimination, recognition would be less slow in coming!' etc. No sooner said than he gets it into his head to steer our reputation, and amend the injustices of mankind. He requires: (1) your photograph, (2) your biography, (3) your complete works, (4) an unpublished manuscript. All of which will appear in a journal of international repute with which he is on very good terms.

And his astonishment when you do not reply.

9 November.

These notes I make each day are a happy miscarriage of the bad things I would otherwise bring into the world.

12 November.

Théâtre de l'Œuvre. *Peer Gynt*. The actress Nau, in despair, wants to commit suicide. Not here! Wait until I am gone. For good or ill, French wit exists, after all. Who among us, even were we capable, would have the temerity to write plays like Ibsen? [...]

It is true that even we experience the urge to write a *Faust*, from time to time, but we hold back. A man from the North does not hold back, and he turns the bourgeois into a prisoner drunk with liberty.

15 November.

Literary discussion. Veber and Gandillot sing the praises of Dickens. I shout for all I am worth that all foreign writers bore me to tears, that there are perhaps some good things here and there, but that to us alone is given perfection, and that I will only tolerate French literature. Capus sides with me.

17 November.

At times in this life I have found myself dancing – but I was by myself.

The happy author. I have worked well, and I am pleased with the result. I put down my pen because night is falling. I muse in the dusk. My wife and child are in the next room, full of life. I have health, success, enough money, not too much.

Good Lord, so *that's* why I am so miserable!

1896

20 November.

Heinrich Heine. Yes, yes, he produces an amusing expression from time to time.

23 November.

In the country, Mme Rostand lets her children play with the village children. Among whom is a little girl called Dry Mouth, who wears no knickers – a real child of air and earth who calls Maurice 'my Prince'. Maurice says a rude word in reply: 'Pig'.

'Ugh!' says Dry Mouth, 'what a horrid thing to say. For which you are going to apologize to me right now, my Prince, and do as I do.'

She makes a genuflection. Maurice, taken aback, does the same, and says to her:

'Does your Maman forbid you from hearing rude words?'

'Yes,' she says. 'I never let one pass me by, and the little coalman uttered one the other day and refused to apologize, so I clouted the bugger.' [...]

Mme Rostand, in need of a valet, interviewed a dozen butlers, in rue Fortuny, courtesy of the small ads in the *Figaro*. They all appeared, present and correct, lined up in the empty drawing-room. One of them said to her:

'Madame, I only troubled to come because Madame has such nice handwriting.'

He draws a fistful of letters from his pocket and says: 'You see, Madame, here are letters which I do not bother to open. Look, Madame, this is not handwriting.'

Another one had left the service of the Duchess d'Uzès because he prefers to be first in a small establishment than second in the house of a duchess. A third had left the employ of some fashionable people because the table was improperly laid.

'Yes, Madame. And if Madame so wishes, one evening when she is not too occupied, I will show her – to divert her and make her laugh – how they laid the table in this house that I was obliged to leave.'

The others were all married and variously demanded (starting with the oldest): an evening off each month, an evening off every two weeks, an evening off every week, and so on, according to age, until the last and youngest – who wanted an evening off every day of the week.

8 December.

Were I to be decorated I would be subject to fewer indignities in life: I have no desire to be decorated.

10 December.

Sarah Bernhardt's routine.

When she descends the winding staircase of a grand house, it is as though she were standing still, while the staircase swirls around her. [...]

I do not know how to help a woman into her wrap. I place Mme Rostand's wrap on her shoulders inside out, and fail to hand her the horn comb properly. I tell her:

'Some day, when we're alone in a corner, you will allow me to kiss your hand, to learn how it is done.'

'Just a little above the wrist,' says she, 'it begins to have savour.' [...]

Sarah is an extraordinary stealer of hearts, so to speak. She may not have talent, but after her day, which is also our day, in which we love and cherish each other, feel renewed and taller – a blessed state of over-excitation – *if* the following day we are still talentless, then we are nothing but cretins. [...]

'You find me silly, don't you?'

'I find you marvellous.'

'I want to be silly today. Do you want to kiss me?'

I do believe that I made her ask her question twice. She kisses me, simply, on both cheeks. I kiss her just a little, on a corner of her mouth, not daring to press. And I say to the Rostands and the rest of them:

'I am blest! Sarah Bernhardt kissed me. I kissed Sarah Bernhardt.'

Imagine the most witless of scribblers. The most talentless. He knows it, he is resigned to it, but sometimes he draws himself up to his full height, with a light in his eyes, and says: 'Ah, if only Sarah were to declaim a single line of mine! The next day I would be famous.'

Imagine the ugliest of men. No one will ever love him. He knows it, he is resigned, but sometimes he dreams: 'Ah, if for a moment I could be near to Sarah, unnoticed in a corner! I would count myself the most beloved of men. I would care nothing for any other woman. They are perfectly pleasant, perfectly lovely, but let us admit that Sarah is genius.'

And every evening there is some fortunate individual who is seeing Sarah act for the first time.

13 December.

To those who say, 'Write us a novel,' I reply that I am not writing a novel. Whatever I produce, I give it to you in my books. It is the year's harvest, so to speak. Tell me if you find it good or bad, but not that you would have preferred something different.

We do not have the same thoughts, but we have thoughts of the same colour.

God: a devil who has created space, in which to fly, but has not given us wings.

16 December.

My morality is as necessary to me as my skeleton.
At a sign from Sarah Bernhardt I would follow her to the ends of the earth – with my wife.

22 December.

This kind of intermittent dialogue which I believed I had invented in *L'Écornifleur* – now I find it already there in the writings of the comtesse de Ségur.

28 December.

In literature, as in billiards, line up your shots.

30 December.

Painters can always claim that their subject is poorly lit.

A duck honourably dead of boredom.

The walls of provincial towns perspire with resentment.

Young lady, your vine leaf has phylloxera.

The clouds pass each other, seeking their places, and line up in battle formation.

Seated beside the empty grate, the cat purrs away like a simmering pot which boils over.

1897

3 January.

To write for children tales of the hunt, as told by the hare.

5 January.

A sensitive savage, when you abandon yourself to your daydreams, how often do you imagine the death of your wife – and burst into tears!

13 January.

Above the bath in Muhlfeld's washroom, a painting by Vallotton. Redoutable females with horrific bottoms, the protruding behinds of hamadryas baboons, hands on their haunches. Coiffures like bunches of twisted grass, touches of green and crushed flowers amidst all the hair. Asked for their opinion, our womenfolk admit to finding it all a little bizarre. One of the joys of being a writer is to be able to say: 'I know nothing about painting; shall we talk about something else?'

I am always being told: 'I have an uncle from whom you

would get loads of ideas!' Or: 'I must introduce you to my cousin, he's a real original!' They offer up to me their entire family. The humblest oyster-basket would be of more use to me.

15 January.

I languish from not being able to go to the moon.

22 January.

Our love for certain women is similar to the warmth we bear towards certain men. It's just that there is more charm and more risk. If we were allowed to kiss the hand of a man without ridicule, to caress the cheek of a man we love, inhale his scent, look at him tenderly, the friendship of men would become dearer to us than the love of women.

An intelligent woman leaves us to our daydreams. I reserve the right to love any woman, just as I would like one day to go to Florence. I do not go to Florence, because I do not have the money, or the time. I do not sleep with this or that woman because I am married, or she is married – but no one can demand that I banish such ideas from my thoughts. They preoccupy me. They take their place inside me. Woman, if you put yourself in the way of my daydreams, woe betide us both! Let them live out their tiny lives and die.

I am more inclined to become a saint than to chase after women. My life, the gravity of my temper, my ambition, my inner thoughts, all of these mark me out as a saintly type; but I am aware that it would take a miracle for me to become a saint. I am at the mercy of the nearest slut, and it frightens me.

You think it vain of me to say I have talent. But what use to me is talent? Genius is what I need; and my modesty is to despair of having genius.

23 January.

I should like to be a saint, but without praying.

28 January.

Valéry, a prodigious talker. Between the Café de la Paix and the *Mercure de France*, an amazing display of his riches of mind, a rare treasure. He brings everything back to mathematics. He would like to create a logarithm table for writers. This is why Mallarmé interests him so much, in whom he finds a precision of syntax. He would like to do for the sentence what has only been done for words: to show its genesis. He despises mere intelligence. He says that brute strength has the right to arrest intelligence and throw it in jail. Too much intelligence causes self-disgust.

'Where I come from, in the Languedoc,' says Robert de Flers, 'the peasant when he makes his will says: "I leave so much to Paul, so much to Pierre, and I keep five hundred francs for myself," meaning that he wants five hundred francs' worth of Masses to be said for his soul.'

Each year they elect a new Jesus. It can be anyone, and everyone must worship him for a year.

1897

31 January.

'Lautrec is very amusing,' says Bernard. 'He is always using the word "technique", but can only have a vague sense of its meaning, for he will say: "Now there is a vase which is the technique of the cup shape," or, of a certain individual, "He is the very technique of jealousy."'

9 February.

There is talk of going to London, where the cost of living is six times higher than Paris. 'So we'll stay for six days instead of thirty-six,' says Bernard. 'The hotels are cheap, so long as you do not sleep in them or eat in them, and that you only enter them – with an innocent air – to use their lavatories.'

Lautrec is waiting for the death of Queen Victoria. As soon as the news arrives, he will make a dash for London to witness a spectacle unique in this century. Allais says she only keeps going by drinking gin.

22 February.

The wit of an Englishwoman: 'I want to live with regrets, not with remorse.'

21 March.

Joy lacks nuance: it is merely a dilation of the heart. The author of a masterpiece and the little tightrope walker balancing on her wire in the circus enjoy the same applause.

4 April.

The dawning of his gift, for a man of letters, is when he needs to convince others that he is misunderstood by his family.

6 April.

I am running the gauntlet of success. I hope to emerge victorious, in other words, disgusted with myself.

8 April.

'I want to be taken for a quadruped,' says the ostrich.

German, my favourite language in which to be silent.

Prudence is merely an attribute: important not to turn it into a virtue.

10 April.

I say good evening to Sarah Bernhardt, who half closes her little llama-eyes in order to make it look as though she did not see me. Decidedly, I am beginning to find the great actress insufferable, as does everyone else. I can only tolerate God himself if He is straightforward and unassuming. Besides, she lives too hard to have the time either to think or to feel.

She gulps down life. It is a sort of gluttony, very disagreeable.

X-rays, a childish plaything. They remind me of the juvenile experiments of my chemistry teacher. A good deal less pretty than a ray of sunlight. Behind the screen, the professor murmurs from time to time, 'Now look at this,' passing different objects in front of the machine – boxes, hands, arms, stuffed animals, a little live dog ... The only thing that is clearly recognizable is a sleeve button.

17 April.

This morning, a letter from Mother, saying that Papa has had an attack of breathlessness, that he himself asked for the doctor, that it is a congestion of the lungs, and to be taken seriously.

I am over thirty-three years of age, and this is the first time I am required to look fixedly at the death of a loved one. At first, it does not register. I try smiling. A congestion of the lungs – that's nothing.

19 April.

He has a familiar gesture. He leans his right elbow on the table, rests his cheek on his hand, and, with the nail of his little finger, probes a buried tooth. I have inherited this tic. I have inherited evasive answers and a fear of enemas. My brother and sister have inherited other tics.

Between us, the words 'filial' and 'paternal' mean little. What has bound us together is a mixture of respect, surprise, and fear. I was always careful to concede that he was different to other men, and always anxious to show that I was not afraid of him.

I pluck the hairs from my nose just as he does, but – being more sedentary – I take more time over it.

14 May.

Marinette says to Papa:

'Have you had a bowel movement today?'

'Oh,' says he, 'every day can't be Sunday.'

He looks at his nails and says: 'They're long, yellow, and black.'

'Shall I cut them for you?'

She cuts them and cleans them, while teasing him: 'Lord, how hard they are!'

'And I have claws on my feet,' says my father. Marinette says she will cut those for him tomorrow. [...]

As Marinette is sponging Papa's face, Maman, from the kitchen, says:

'Oh, if you would only take advantage of his being sick to tidy him up. He lives in a state of shameful filth. Thank heavens, at least I take care of his linen! He has only to open the closet and take out a shirt, or a pair of drawers.'

Papa no longer even laughs up his sleeve. What is there between those two? A lot of small things, and then nothing. He hates and despises her. Especially, he despises her, and I do believe he is also a little afraid of her.

As for her, she is probably not aware. She resents her humiliations, his obstinate silences. But were he to talk to her, she would throw herself on his neck in a flood of tears, then immediately go and repeat what he said to the entire village. But it is thirty years since he has said anything.

1897

21 May.

Maurice has taken the revolver out of the drawer of the night table, saying he wants to clean it. Papa, who is feeling well tonight, says:

'He says that, but he's lying. He is afraid I might kill myself. If I wanted to kill myself I would not use an implement you can only cripple yourself with.'

'Will you stop talking like that!' says Marinette.

'No, I would go the whole hog and get my rifle.'

'You'd do better to get an enema,' I tell him.

22 May.

Papa still has his mind, slow-running and clear. My own, when I talk to him, no longer seems so sharp. I am always afraid of saying something *untrue*, and of expressing it badly, so that he must think: 'Why are they always talking about my son? I don't see anything special about him.' He talks in a low voice, to spare his chest, and each of his carefully chosen words is a little painful to the listener. As soon as Maman opens the door, he stops. She comes in because she thinks he is about to say something that she would like to know. Dragging her bad leg, she goes to the closet, opens it, touches the pile of linen, pretends to be looking for something, listens, and removes nothing. She walks around the table, moves a newspaper. At last, she finds a cup and carries it out. She has learnt nothing. As soon as the door closes, Papa, who has been slowly walking about the room, completes his sentence in the same key in which he started it.

8 June.

Papa keeps his mayor's sash in a little red box that once contained starched shirt-collars from Le Bon Marché. When he has a marriage ceremony to perform, he takes the box to the *mairie*, places it on the table, and merely opens it. If they stand on tiptoe, the wedding pair and their witnesses can see the sash. – 'It's enough,' says Papa. He has never worn it; consequently there are innumerable couples who are never entirely sure if they are properly married.

12 June.

Papa and the cupping. Six claret glasses are already lined up on the table, but the doctor brings proper cupping-glasses and Maman takes hers away.

Papa turns over on his right side. The doctor lights a piece of paper at a candle, puts the paper into a glass, applies the glass to his back. Immediately, the skin swells up, in the manner of a bump on the forehead. The procedure is repeated with six little glasses, and Papa remains fifteen minutes with the glasses on his back.

He looks like a liquorice-water vendor.

His back with its russet tips of fire, the dark pattern of vesicatories, the violet moons left by the cupping glasses, and further down, at the loins, an enormous mole, and, still lower, a few long, sparse hairs, as fine as the hair on his head.

Empty buttocks with folds like the folds of empty sacks.

When he sleeps, the end of his nose, his cheekbones and his nails turn purple. The blood no longer reaches them.

He always washed his head in a glass of water, using his cupped hands.

He always brushed his hair furiously.

He never wore either rings or braces.

He never put on a nightshirt, but wore his day shirt to bed.

He always pared his nails with a pocket knife.

He never went to bed without reading his paper or without blowing out his candle.

He never put on his drawers and his trousers separately.

13 June.

I am a realist who is unnerved by reality.

18 June.

Papa goes into the garden to sit under the hazel bushes, and does not notice that right by him there are a warbler's nest, a chaffinch nest, a goldfinch nest. How the sap has sunk in him!

19 June.

Half past one. Death of my father.

You could say of him, 'This was only a man, only the mayor of an impoverished little village,' and yet speak of his death as though it were the death of Socrates. I do not reproach myself for not having loved him enough; I reproach myself for not having understood him.

After lunch, I was writing a few letters. The porch bell rings. It is Marie, Papa's little maid, come to say that he is asking for me.

She does not know why. I stand up, just a little surprised. Marinette, perhaps more worried than I, says: 'I'll go over.' Without haste, I put on my shoes, put some air in my tyres.

On arriving at the house, I see Maman in the street. She screams: 'Jules! Oh! Jules!' and 'Why did he lock himself in!' She looks like a madwoman. Still barely more excited than before, I try to open the door. Impossible. I call – no answer – I guess nothing. I imagine that he felt unwell, or is in the garden.

I ram the door with my shoulder, and eventually it gives.

Smoke and a smell of powder. I find myself crying out: 'Oh, Papa, Papa! What's this! Well look what you've done! Oh! Oh!' And still I do not believe it; he is surely joking. I do not believe his white face, his open mouth, or that dark patch, near the heart.

Borneau, who was returning from Corbigny, and is the next to enter the room, says to me:

'He must be forgiven. He was suffering too much.'

Forgiven? For what? What a bizarre thought! Now that I have grasped everything, I feel nothing. I go into the courtyard, I say to Marinette, who has lifted Maman from the ground:

'It is over. Come along!'

Marinette enters, erect, pale, and looks glancingly in the direction of the bed. She cannot breathe, opens the top of her bodice. She is able to weep. She says, referring to Maman:

'Don't let her in. She is out of her mind.'

We both stand there. He is lying on his back, legs outstretched, the top of his body inclined, head back, mouth and eyes open. Between his legs, his rifle; his walking stick between the bed and the wall: his hands, empty, have let go of both stick and rifle. They are still warm, relaxed. A little above the waist, a black place, resembling a small burnt-out fire.

1897

28 June.

On the whole, his death has added to my pride.

On 21 June, at one o'clock, the coffin is taken out through the garden so that my mother and sister do not hear it. People are standing about on the street. Most of them are wearing red *immortelles* in their buttonholes. M. Hérisson is present. I say:

'We are especially obliged to you for being here today.'

I go into the street. I feel that everyone is watching me, that after my father I am the main actor in the ceremony, so I must cut a figure. I feel it acutely.

We move off. The ten municipal councillors take turns to bear the coffin. You can hear at each step the metal handles knocking against the wood.

We pass in front of the *mairie* and then the church. The sun is warm on our heads. Latecomers are arriving, from all directions. In one carriage, old Rigaud, mayor of Marigny, eighty-four years old, and his son who seems older than he.

The cemetery. The pit is there, in a corner, by the road.

M. Billiard, in a clear voice, reads his written eulogy, looking at me after each sentence, says 'constitutions' instead of 'citizens', then stops abruptly: a page has been lost. Long silence, whiff of malice in the air. He improvises or recites from memory the ending. M. Hérisson comes after him, very moved, says a few words. During all of which I keep passing my hand over my head. The sun is making me feel faint.

They wait. Nothing more. I should like to explain the meaning of this death, but nothing comes. They throw the *immortelles* into the pit. A little earth topples in. No lining up to shake hands. People start to drift away. I stay put, I stay put. A miserable ham actor! I feel as if I am overacting on purpose. Why? You wretch. Are none of my other feelings truly mine, just like my sadness?

None of those people looked too happy about taking part, out of decency, in a ceremony without a priest. No doubt it was the first civil burial in Chitry.

3 July.

Sometimes, in a macabre mimicry, I stop in the middle of the road and open my mouth the way his was open as he lay on the bed.

For the first time since he was buried, I passed near the cemetery. I stopped mechanically. So there he is, a few steps away, on the other side of the wall, flat on his back and already being eaten.

He had shown no signs of decrepitude, so it's as if he killed himself in his prime, out of a strength greater than mine.

9 July.

Along the road, a flock of geese who seem to be guarding a little girl. Further on, another flock guarding another little girl, who lifts her head and is an old woman. The goose acting as leader has a small stick attached to his neck. It looks like a small pole, to keep him steady, but it is to stop him from pushing through the hedges and causing damage in the fields.

1897

10 July.

His cemetery. Poppies, tall grasses where the larks will find shelter. A very long worm comes out of the loosened earth. A few ants. At each moment I forget that he is there, that I am walking over him.

Flowers on a grave soon turn ugly, like old signboards above pothouses.

13 July.

His grave does not sadden me, no doubt because he is there. But when, from the road, I look at the house in which he killed himself, his house, and I don't see him, from behind, sitting on the wall with his arms crossed, and I don't see his white beard under the straw hat, I am sad that he is no longer here.

Maurice says to me:

'One of these days, I'll fool you. I'll sit in his place on the wall.'

And what if he had missed? What if he had only maimed himself? What if he had not had the strength to take that second shot? What if he had screamed at me: 'Finish me off!' What then would I have done?

Would I have been brave enough to take his rifle and finish him off, or to choke him to death by hugging him?

16 July.

My father (21 May, redrafted). Approaching his bed to embrace him, I put my foot right into his chamber pot. During the time it takes to see what I've done and say 'Shit!', the kiss goes cold on my lips. My surprise at seeing him better.

'We ought to air the room with a warming pan,' he said, 'or burn a little sugar to chase away the smell.'

'You get used to it,' says Maurice.

'You also get used to the smell of sugar,' says my father softly.

The voices of old men, invertebrate voices, without any edges.

21 July.

Not yet, obviously! But I have a suspicion that, sooner or later, in a moment of absolute disgust, or what Baudelaire calls 'dull incuriosity', I shall do as he did. Little empty cartridge-shell, staring at me like an eyeless socket.

Never let it be said: 'His father was braver than he!'

24 July.

Papon, the ranger of Chitry, died yesterday evening at 10 p.m. He would have much preferred to keep working, scything his wheat himself, his patch not worth what it would cost for another man to cut it.

When he was forced to admit that, clearly, he could no longer keep working, he said to Marinette:

'I think it will end badly.'

As soon as they are sick, they want to be dead. A way of life so sad that one dare not make literature out of it. When they fall ill, they say to their family: 'There it is! From now on I'll only be a burden on you!'

And the pharmacy! When you think that the well-off, meaning those who eat soup with bacon every day, can afford eight francs for a bottle of medicine . . .

They borrow a thousand francs to buy a bit of land, and will never do more than repay the interest on this loan. It is a debt for life. And they are far too trusting of the notary, without whom they dare not sign anything, and yet the notary is the first to take his cut.

We take exception to their vices, their failings, their shiftiness. To the fact that they drink, that they beat their wives. We forget that destitution gives them rights.

What astonished Papon most about my father's death, was that he should kill himself despite being so well cared for.

'If I were half as well looked after as the late M. Renard,' he said to Marinette, 'you'd never see the end of me.'

My father had a heart, but his heart was not a home.

26 July.

Here, when someone dies, you burn their straw; as a sanitary measure. But the canvas is kept, of course. Only the straw is burnt, the rest of the mattress and bedding are untouched.

27 July.

Even a rock has moss. My father had no tenderness, to speak of, and he never said thank you.

30 July.

My father. The following day I had to get up from the table to go away and weep. It was the first time, in the twenty hours I had sat by him. Floods of tears; I had not been able to squeeze a single tear hitherto.

A fine death. I do believe that if he had killed himself in front of me I should have made no attempt to stop him. We must not diminish the merit of his act. He killed himself, not because he suffered, but because he did not wish to be alive other than in good health.

He should have confided in me. We might have discussed his death in the manner of Socrates and his friends. Perhaps the thought occurred to him. But I know perfectly well that I'd have behaved like a fool. I'd have said: 'What! Are you crazy! Stop worrying me, let's change the subject.'

1 August.

The death of my father – as though I had written a good book.

5 August.

I am a man who comes from the Centre of France, sheltered from the mists of the North and the hot blood of the South. My cicada is the grasshopper, and there is nothing mythological about my grasshoppers. They are not made of gold. I pick them in the meadows, swaying on the end of a blade of grass. I remove their thighs and use them as bait when I go fishing with a rod and line.

6 September.

God knows everything. He will refuse to open the pearly gates to me if I make a grammatical error.

17 September.

I used not to like hunting and saw it as a barbarous pastime. Now I like it, so as to please my father. Each partridge I kill, I glance in his direction and he understands. In the evening on my way home, if I pass the cemetery I say: 'Guess what, old boy, bagged six today!'

What it is to throttle a partridge! To close your grip on its throat, feel between your fingers the tiny fluttering life!

But if I come home with an empty bag I make sure not to pass the cemetery gate.

28 September.

Return to Paris. My father and I. We did not love each other outwardly. We did not cling together by our branches: we were attached by our roots.

29 September.

Some men give the impression of having married solely to prevent their wives from marrying other men.

30 September.

Old age begins when you find yourself saying 'I have never felt so young'.

Mourning is so tiresome. At every moment you must remind yourself that you are sad.

'Why do you keep writing about the death of your father?'

'You would prefer me to write about Venice? I have never been to Venice!'

My soul is an old chamber pot in which an eye is sleeping.

6 November.

The star is hiding. It takes me for a poet. It is afraid I might make it rhyme.

30 November.

And to think that my father, who slaughtered himself like a hero, was always afraid of going to the dentist.

8 December.

We always say that we are popular in Germany, to console ourselves for not being read in France.

1897

15 December.

Music frightens me. I feel as though I were in a tiny boat adrift on immense waves. What sets me against music, of which I know nothing, is that so many petty provincial magistrates are fanatical about it. What is it that can get such people so worked up?

16 December.

Alphonse Daudet is dead. After you left he would always undress you in front of those who stayed. By the time you got to the foot of the stairs you were entirely naked.

We are too preoccupied with death. We should try to ignore it when it passes by: it might come less often. It is of no importance.

A small mystery. I often asked him for his portrait: he would never give it to me.

23 December.

The daydreams I have, as if my unconscious in its entirety were chasing out my conscious self and installing itself in its place. I do not know them, these images that so suddenly intervene. But since I cannot deny their existence – they are there, inside of me – I must accept that they belong to another me, and that I am double.

28 December.

Cyrano. Flowers, nothing but flowers, all the bouquets in the world for our great dramatic poet! Another masterpiece is born.

Let us rejoice. Let us rest on our laurels. Let us wander, from theatre to theatre, and sit through the latest rubbish: it cannot disturb us. Because whenever we choose, we can revisit this masterpiece. We can lean against it, take shelter inside it, escape from others inside it, even from ourselves.

How true, that fever is the proof of health! How happy I am! How alive I feel! The friendship of Rostand consoles me for having been born too late to belong to the intimate circle of Victor Hugo.

I would even swear that, being of sound mind, I believe myself inferior to this fine, lucid genius that is Edmond Rostand.

The superiority of Rostand: he overwhelms us and we have nothing to say in return; but if *we* had written his *Cyrano*, he would have found something to say to us.

1898

1 January.

So where am I? Soon to be thirty-four, a small reputation, let us say – a small name which nothing prevents from becoming a bigger name. (Others think it, but I know it, alas.) I could make a lot of money, but I make only a little. A year since the last book. A barren year, not counting *Le Plaisir de Rompre*. It is true that I have the excuse of a father's death, but this scarcely accounts for my torpor. No moral progress, far from it! I have merely perfected my egotism. I have demonstrated to Marinette that her happiness depends on my freedom. Do I even love my children? I do not rightly know. They move me when I set eyes on them, but I do not seek them out. They serve to make me feel moved by myself. A generalized good-will, which it would pain me to direct usefully at anyone in particular. Not sensual enough to chase after women, I always feel that the first that comes along could make me do whatever she pleases.

Friends but no friend. I have more or less lost Rostand, and his success will not bring us any closer. I do nothing for anyone. Which is perhaps the best proof that I amount to something. They can only like me out of genuine esteem.

Habitually in a vicious temper. After a few steps in the street I become unbearable. Happily I do not go out too often.

I have an old soul, just as my father was old in body. What do I wait for, before doing away with myself in turn? What is more, I think I am becoming a miser, and imagine that I am paying for too many carriages. I am even sure of it.

2 January.

To punish us for our laziness, there are our failures – but also the successes of others.

3 January.

As for Rostand – Rostand who arrived under his own steam, not by way of the little reviews but by way of the big ones; who prefers society to editorial offices; who does not consume bocks in the brasseries with the bohemians, but dines at the houses of the rich; who prefers theatre directors to theatre critics, Sarah Bernhardt to Lugné-Poe ... Rostand describes for us a visit he paid to Mlle Lucie Faure. She had asked him for a sonnet, for a good cause, and he brought her his work. She received him very simply, in a small salon full of marvellous antique curios. Mme Barthou was present, perfectly charming. Suddenly in walked Félix Faure, paying his daughter a visit. He was on his way back from hunting, and wore a small soft hat. He excused his appearance, sat down and said: 'Monsieur Rostand, good day!' He was enchanting. It is no wonder that the Tsar adores him. He is a consummate performer. He is what Europe has that is closest to Louis XIV. And then he stood up, saluted the company, and left to attend to his toilette. This gentleman must go to a lot of trouble over his appearance. He ought to be President of the Republic, which, since the Revolution, has taken not a single step in the direction of good sense or liberty.

9 January.

Sarah saying to Barbier:
'It is very good, your play, if only it were in verse.'
'Very well!' says Barbier, and brings it back to her in verse.
'Ah, if only it were in verse!'
'But it is in verse,' says Barbier.
'Yes, but in different verse.'

14 January.

Flaubert was so benevolent that he took all novices seriously.
'Write your sentence on a slate,' he said to Le Roux. 'If it is pretty to look at, then it is a good sentence. If it shocks the eye, it is no good.'
A theory, of sorts, though Flaubert could do better when he tried.
The admiration of Le Roux for Flaubert is touching. He knows all of it by heart. He should really recite some to us more often.

16 January.

He has been in love with the same woman for three years. For whom he has perpetrated every sort of idiocy. He has wrecked his life, ruined himself, had himself dishonourably discharged from his regiment on account of his lies, narrowly escaping hard labour. He has committed all the follies of which he was capable. And still he is in love. He is finished: he will never be anything except a lover. He is pale, a wallower in the mire; at twenty-three years of age he already seems old. A constant plaintive whinge in his voice: 'Ah, Monsieur, if you only knew!'

'You want to be admired,' he says, 'it is the goal of your life. I want to be loved; it is my only ideal.'

But my ideal is even more exhausting than his, because it makes me feel I'm forty.

21 January.

La Ville Morte, by D'Annunzio. To be considered as poetry, rather as gold is considered a precious metal – merely by convention.

When a poet puts the word 'gold' in a line, whatever the line, he is reassured as to its value. The line is already worth its weight ... in gold. As for other stale comparisons – 'flash of diamond ... pure as water ... fine as the sea sand' – it is a long time since anyone has resorted to such threadbare fustian.

31 January.

Poverty. My wife is the charitable one. As for me, I wrap myself in quills, like a hedgehog. It confuses them. The priest's remark: 'The devil has married an angel.' This suits both my sense of irony and my attitude to the poor. They accept charity more willingly from her, because they imagine that she does it without my knowing. They think they are having a joke at my expense. 'He never gives us anything,' they say, and they hold out their hands brazenly. They avenge themselves for my severity. The alms they accept are stolen goods, so to speak.

My independence has its price. I tell people I have a horror of banquets and grand dinners: consequently I am not invited to them. I am invited separately, out of consideration. Otherwise I might put my foot in it. They are wary of my plain-speaking.

Invited alone, I can have things my way, and the meal is soon over. Soup, two dishes, no choices, and a dessert. I am kept sober. I am here for the conversation. Quick, clear the table! Let us go into the salon for coffee and get down to some talk.

2 February.

The moon behind the cloud, narrowing slowly, like the eye of a cat.

12 February.

When I see a woman's breast, I see double.

18 February.

This evening, at the *Revue blanche*. Everyone is in the grip of the Dreyfus affair. We would sacrifice wives, daughters, fortunes. Thadée, who brings the news, becomes a person of consequence by dint of association.

'I dined yesterday,' says Mallarmé, 'with Poincaré, who is

for Zola – without being for Dreyfus – and who kept saying gloomily, "I fear war!"'

'He should have himself disinfected!' said Léon Blum.

'Why war?' I asked.

'We were already on the verge of it during the trial,' said Mallarmé. 'We escaped by a whisker. The German ambassador brought everything to a standstill. But now, Wilhelm is getting more and more wound up. If his wife didn't hold him back . . .'

'That seems a little simplistic,' I say. 'But I can understand the frustration of Wilhelm. First of all the French tell him: "The Russians are with us. Come and join us. The time is right!" And then the tall stories about artillery pieces stolen and sold to the Germans. You can see why Wilhelm feels the need to shout at us: "You bore me with your tales of stolen artillery! I don't need your secret artillery to beat you: I have my own armies. I'll show you!"'

21 *February*.

I never noticed that the compliments I was paid were not sincere.

23 *February*.

Zola is condemned to a year of prison and fined a thousand francs. And I want to declare, here and now:

That I am sick at heart, sick to the bottom of my heart, at the sentencing of Émile Zola. [. . .]

And I swear that Zola is innocent.

And I declare too:

That I have no respect for our army chiefs, whom a long peace has rendered too haughty;

That I once took part in manoeuvres, on three occasions, and that everything seemed to me to be disorder, braggartry, obfuscation and infantile behaviour. Of the three different officers who turned me into a stupefied corporal, the captain was a mediocre careerist, the lieutenant an insignificant little womanizer, the second lieutenant a respectable young man who must long since have quit the service. [. . .]

Zola is a fortunate man. He has found his *raison d'être*, and can thank his pathetic jurors who have inadvertently crowned him with a year of heroism.

28 February.

'Zut!' says Baïe.
'What?'
'Nothing. It's English.'

1 March.

Mallarmé. Untranslatable, even into French.

8 March.

Baïe. When she gets cross with her cat, she addresses it as '*vous*'.

'Was it Flaubert who put his trousers on backwards?' she asks.

15 March.

In the evening, I catch up with Guitry who is dining with the actor Noblet, chez Joseph, who owns a restaurant on the rue Marivaux. This Joseph carves a duck as though he were playing the violin, and he serves us a *fine* of champagne cognac that is so expensive, he cannot sell it and prefers to pour it for his friends.

30 March.

Ibsen. *An Enemy of the People*. Séverine wearing mahogany shavings on her head. Thadée Natanson, Ibsen's master of ceremonies. A play which is perfectly lucid, in which, on the pretext of a humble municipal spa, the most outrageous ideas are perpetrated. A play that seems as if exactly copied from the Zola affair. Ibsen is applauded, but it is a case of mistaken identity.

31 March.

Dinner with Rostand.
'So, Renard, what would you do in my place, after *Cyrano*?'
'Me? I would rest for a decade.'
Where he works best is on a train, or even in a hackney carriage. The movement agitates his mind, like a basket full of ideas.

1 April.

At La Gloriette.
As sad as a widow watching an autumn landscape through the window.

A pregnant sow, red, covered in filth. Her swollen nipples touch the ground. Now there is a mother! She commands respect like those women who, on doctor's orders, take the air along the Champs Élysées, expensively dressed and preceded by a magnificent belly.

April.

At the cemetery. I try to imagine the horrible thing that is my father's face now, and I feel the grimace made by my own face.

Just a little fame would do for me, just enough so that I do not seem an imbecile in my own village.

The duck tries to jump over a wall and get through a hedge. Halfway up the wall, she falls back heavily. She does not insist: she goes and fetches the drake. Together, heads erect, they examine the wall, look for an opening in the hedge. From time to time, they abandon the attempt, go the long way around by the field, nibble a little grass, and return to the fray.

The duck gets halfway into the hedge; but it is too dense: she abandons the idea.

They go round by the meadow, wasting their day and mine.

With their jerky good-day, good-day, good-day.

It is a murky business. And would take a comic genius to sort it out.

You think they will fly off, but no, they are not so bold.

Do not ask me to be kind; just ask me to act as though I were.

Such calm! I can hear all my thoughts.

A willow tree with a hairdo like Alphonse Daudet.

Porel used to say:
'As far as actors are concerned, friends are a poor public.'
'And sometimes the public is a poor public,' said Capus.

27 April.

I look at Fantec. He is nearly ten years old. When he is fifteen I will not yet be forty, and we have almost nothing in common.

I don't need him to read my books, nor to admire me.

And I can be useful to him only indirectly, which is to say I need to make money so that he can pursue his studies and become whoever he wants to be.

I feel only two or three particular obligations towards him, though these are in conflict with my mature reflections: I have to be an honourable father whose name, in society, is not an invitation to ridicule; I have to go on writing bad plays which will enable me to pay for his education. The rest is not his business. He may laugh if he likes at the inventions of the author of the *Histoires Naturelles*. And he in turn (like the rest of the universe) only interests me as raw material for literature.

I have also perhaps the obligation, which I find easier, of making his mother happy so that he will be happy through her.

In other words, he and I have only an indirect relation. This causes me wonder and saddens me a little as I write these lines, though doubtless I shall give it no further thought this evening.

9 May.

Inspiration is perhaps merely the joy of writing: it does not precede writing.

20 May.

The heart of a woman is a peach-stone. You bite into the peach enthusiastically, and suddenly you break a tooth.

21 May.

Human stupidity. A tautology: it is only humans who are stupid.

26 May.

At the Paris Salon exhibition. As with the Opéra-Comique, I had not been for ten years. Only the statue of Balzac by Rodin catches my attention. Seen from behind, a three-quarter view at twenty yards, the attitude is striking. And the hollow eyes, the screwed-up face, the narrow forehead, a man doing battle with his work smock, the whole thing is impressive. You could say of this statue what Mme Victorine de Chatenay said of Joubert: 'A soul which found itself joined to a body by accident, and was trying to deal with the consequences as best it could.'

29 May.

Hauptmann's *Les Tisserands*. Pierre Loti. With an air almost of religious zeal Antoine announced: 'Loti is coming this evening.'

Rings on his fingers, a tie-pin that is too large, too golden: it looks like a royal tiara. A youthful appearance, perhaps too youthful – a little faded. [. . .]

He does not mention my books. No doubt because he is an Academician and an officer of the Légion d'Honneur, I must talk to him about his books. I say that his entire oeuvre has had a great influence on my sensibility. (Why not!)

'Which of your books is your own favourite?'

'Oh, I do not know,' he replies. 'Once I have finished a book I no longer think of it. I have never re-read a single one of them.'

He insists with a special emphasis on being presented to 'Mme Jules Renard'. To him she is an unknown woman, after all, and from every woman he expects something new. Marinette, embarrassed, barely looks at him. But she sees at once what I cannot see.

An exquisite and elaborate courtesy, which forces me into an awkward show of manners. A few white hairs in the moustache. The hair of a young man. Large, slightly withered ears and the eyes – how to describe them?

'Cosmetic! He was made-up, like a woman,' Marinette tells me after we leave. 'His eyelashes are made-up, his eyes are made-up, his hair glistens, his lips are painted. He does not even dare to close his mouth; and those white hairs in his moustache, they are there for effect, to make you think that all the rest is natural.'

And I had seen nothing.

A signature as elegant as the whip-lash of the coachman at one of our great houses.

'Is it Sunday in every country?' asks Baïe.

12 June.

La Gloriette. I listen to the toad, from whom there escapes at regular intervals a note of watery exclamation, a sonorous drop of sadness. It does not seem to come from the earth: you would guess it was the complaint of a bird perched on a tree. It is the obstinate lament of the entire landscape, dripping with rain. A dog's bark, the sound of a door, and the toad falls silent. Then starts up again: '*Ou! Ou! Ou!*' But that is not it. There is a consonant just before this syllable, something glottal in the throat, a lightly aspirated *h*, a bit like the sound of a bubble bursting on the surface of a pond.

It is other things too. It is the sighing of a small soul, infinitely subdued.

And because no one ever replies, no fellow soul out there, in the end it falls completely silent.

18 June.

I cannot say that I would feel flattered, if posthumously some imbecile were to say: 'For me, who knew him well, he was far better than his books.'

22 June.

Michelet tries too hard to make Nature poetic. It is not necessary. Nature mocks any attempt to overstate her case, and, in spite of Michelet's efforts, she slips his grasp. Try reading this aloud to a group of peasants: 'That ringing voice of the lark, full of authority, is a signal to the harvesters. Time to go, says Father: do you not hear the lark?' The peasants would be a little taken aback. None of them has ever received such a signal: none of them would ever have obeyed.

11 July.

No one will ever prevent me from feeling moved when I look at a field, when I walk up to my knees through the oats that spring up behind me. Could any thought be as fine as a blade of grass?

I don't give a straw for my country, taken as a whole: but my local patch moves me to tears. The German emperor cannot take this blade of grass from me.

20 July.

The wisdom of the nations: an imbecilic old crone.

23 July.

The indignation of satire is unnecessary. It is enough to show things as they are. They are ridiculous enough of themselves.

1898

Such is our egotism that, in a storm, we believe the thunder tolls only for us.

From her window, my mother sees Marinette approaching. She goes and sits in the middle of the kitchen and starts to cry, so that Marinette will find her in tears.

'Goodness! What is this all about, Maman?'

'Thoughts . . . they come into my head.'

What thoughts? No means of knowing. We are to guess that they are thoughts of suicide. Certainly, something is troubling her. Furious at not having been invited to my lecture on Michelet, she said to Marie Pierry: 'You will get a bad reputation, mixing with those characters. You know the priests don't care for that sort of talk!'

To Marinette she said: 'I heard it was so beautiful!'

Through Philippe, she learns that I have eaten two or three cherries.

'I'm not surprised! He loved them so much when he was little! He used to smear them all over himself. There! Bring him a basketful! Poor Jules, how happy he'll be!'

Death is comforting: it delivers us from thoughts of death.

1 August.

One ear of wheat to another:

'Watch how straight I hold my head!'

'No wonder,' says the other. 'You have dropped your grains, and your head is empty.'

As long as a man has not explained to himself the secret of the universe, he has no right to feel satisfied.

A blind faith can only displease God.

8 August.

Go outside and smoke a cigarette of air.

I love my village so much that I do not like to see strangers arriving in it.

A swallow, the wind's favourite toy.

15 August.

Pastorals. There are no witches here: the peasants do not believe in spells. There are a few sinister-looking types, but then poverty disfigures everyone.

This old woman with the enormous stomach: no dark business there, no work of the devil. The worst scenario is that she may be hiding under her apron a few vegetables stolen from the fields.

Turkeys with the colouring of constipated Englishwomen.

There is nothing like a disciple for showing us our faults.

I would like to be read by the minority, but known to the majority.

The assurance with which men give names to stars.

It is merely ridiculous to be deaf, but tragic to be blind. Thus do we measure the difference between visible Nature and Man, who speaks.

Why should it be more difficult to die, that is, to go from life to death, than to be born: in other words, to go from death to life?

An implement that has never been replaced and rarely improved upon: the plough.

1 October.

The pig with his cap always over his eyes.

Between the shepherd and his dog, there is only a difference of humanity, a gap which could be jumped by a flea.

Montaigne is heavy going, it has to be said.

A happy life, with tints of despair, such is mine.

Pigeons. Their flight sounds like the smothered laughter of girls, or of nuns in a convent.

The Loire, a great river of sand, occasionally dampened.

If truth lies at the bottom of a well, I will throw myself into the well.

I have never looked at a painting. I make no boast of it. However, I make a point of it. I limit myself as far as possible: deaf to music, blind to art. I think we are all born with a generalized genius which we must find a way to shake off. Nothing is easier, I think, than to be on familiar terms with all the arts, and I endeavour to limit myself to one.

4 November.

A young person is someone who has not yet told a lie.

I throw myself at your feet, Madame, provided there is a cushion there.

6 November.

It may be said of almost all works of literature that they are too long.

9 November.

Léon Blum explains, precisely and with a wealth of examples, the absurdity of an Anglo-French war. It is charming to watch, this beardless youth who might be crazy, but who brings luminous considerations to bear upon a murky subject. All external factors derive from internal factors. France has no reason to fight with England, other than the ministerial instability of one Lord Salisbury, who wants to consolidate his position, just as all wars have motives of this kind. It is shameful.

The fear of a fall from power suffices for a politician to send thousands of men to have their throats cut.

14 November.

Every evening I lead my sensibilities home like a flock of sheep.

19 November.

God himself does not believe in our God.

28 November.

Re-reading myself – a sort of suicide.

29 November.

She writes articles against hunting, and wears a hat made from the feet, beaks and wings of birds.

I always feel like saying to Music: 'None of it is true! You are lying!'

15 December.

Our true opinion of a work is an average of what we tell the author and what we say to our friends.

23 December.

I am of the uncouth sort, who at table say thank you to servants and prefer a forkful of beetroot to a truffle.

26 December.

'In the kitchens,' says a maid in a grand establishment, 'we have a new chef and he knows everything. He told us that mankind is descended from Darwin.'

1899

1 January.

La Gloriette. On rising I resolve to give up most things for this year, and make a start at lunch – by stuffing myself with roast goose and chestnuts followed by *galettes de plomb*.

2 January.

Pleasures do not give me pleasure.

I was born a village mayor.

There is such a wind coming down the chimney that if you put your hand to the fire, your palm is scorched while the back of your hand freezes.

5 January.

Baudelaire: 'The soul of wine was singing in the bottle.' A perfect example of that false poetry which concerns itself with substituting what is not there for what is there. For the true artist, wine sitting in a bottle is truer and more interesting than the soul of wine or the soul of a bottle, since there is no need to bestow a soul upon an object which is getting by perfectly well without one.

6 January.

Every man has in his heart a barrel organ which refuses to stay quiet.

7 January.

There are no synonyms. There are only the right words, and a good writer knows them.

La Fontaine. Individually, his animals are true, but their relation to each other is false. The carp has indeed the air of a gossip, with his back hunched like an old woman, but the carp does not go for endless promenades with her crony the pike; she flees her as a mortal enemy.

As for me, don't worry, I am fairly content to be inferior to my work.

I am sure that my cat is not thinking; nonetheless, it looks as though it were thinking.

A sunbeam in a darkened room. Full of dust motes. Nothing dirtier than a sunbeam.

9 February.

As soon as you compliment a woman on her looks, she thinks herself intelligent.

11 February.

They compliment you on a book by saying: 'It is reprinting.'

At night, I often think I hear the cock crow. The next morning, I ask Philippe if he heard it. He says no, and this troubles me.

To describe a peasant, you should not use words he would not understand.

The cat is the living principle of furniture.

20 February.

'My dear sir, your antipathy does not bother me. I am even convinced that, were I to send you my latest book, with a handsome dedication, you would discover that I have talent.'

7 March.

Sows have under their bellies a waistcoat with a double row of buttons.

21 March.

To be original, it suffices to imitate writers who are no longer in fashion.

14 April.

For a writer who has been working, to read is like getting into a carriage after a tiring walk.

The languid melancholy of working on a Sunday, when others are idling.

17 April.

The ideal: a precise dream.

19 April.

Bernard, who walks around with a cheap five-cents edition of Montaigne. Before he enters a street urinal, he knocks on the corrugated metal door.

Poil de Carotte. I have never been able to take a resolute step without my brother bursting into laugher. Hence my humble, colourless existence.

I do not have an ivory tower, merely an ivory notebook.

To snore is to sleep at the top of one's voice.

1899

24 April.

I can hear my beard growing.

When I married, I duly brought my young wife into the family. My father looked around for something to do in her honour. He decided to replace some of the roof tiles on his house; then he gave up on the idea.

At the zoo. The elephants draw near to each other, link trunks, then blow into each other's mouths as if checking for bad breath. Their sighs would swell a sail. Then they dance, with their heads rather than their feet, in honour of their gentleman visitor. All that flabby mass, and then the little eye, like an eyelet in a great sack.

1 May.

We put all that we have into our first book. It only remains for us to root out our vices and cultivate our virtues – next time round.

There are storytellers and there are writers. You can tell any story you like; you cannot write whatever you like: you write only yourself.

20 May.

It is touching to see Léon Blum with his old blind aunt, as gracious as Antigone. He serves her, describes each dish for her, cuts her meat. Blind for the past thirty-five years, she turns her face in the direction of whoever speaks. Her wrinkled visage is as pale as white linen that is a little creased. A young girl serves as her travelling companion and reads to her. She is interested by everything she cannot see, which astonishes the rest of us, who think we see everything.

2 June.

It is not a question of being first, but of being unique.

Think of the perfect couplet that Molière would have put into the mouth of his Alceste, against patriotism!

14 June.

At the bottom of all patriotism there is war – which is why I am no patriot.

Behind me, the cuckoo sings, mysterious, invisible, disreputable. It stands accused of leaving its eggs, one by one, in the nests of whitethroat or robin, nightingale or wagtail, thrush or blackbird. What a crime! And what about you? Do you never leave your young in other people's beds? Except that you lack the honesty to shout 'Cuckoo!' to announce the fact.

What's this? A purse! No, just a mole that a mower has killed and thrown onto the path.

1899

20 June.

Yesterday, anniversary of father's death. Were it not for Marinette I'd have forgotten.

My mother, who is in bed, has the priest say a Mass. So, three or four old dears listen to a priest praying for the repose of my father's soul.

Marinette and I bring him a wreath, rather heavy, made out of glazed earthenware. We give our dead metal flowers, metal which lasts.

It is less cruel never to visit the dead than to stop visiting them after a while.

I have my faults like everyone else; except that I get nothing out of them.

23 June.

Philippe, when he digs a hole, worries that he might turn up human bones. He says that in the old days they buried the dead everywhere.

24 June.

Several times, in my dreams, I have invented the dendrometer, a device for measuring the height of trees.

25 June.

The young girls of Chaumot all want to go to Paris. Those who are too shy to say 'Paris' say 'the city'. They want to make money in order to get married. As they don't know how to do anything, they add that they are willing to do anything, that it is all the same to them. They have pleated blouses and small brooches, are bare-headed, have worn-out shoes, clean hands and dirty nails, open faces and pink cheeks, though their teeth are a worry.

28 June.

When I used to see my father walking from one window to the other, stooped, silent, hands behind his back, a deep expression on his face, I used to ask myself: 'What is he thinking?' Today I know, because I walk to and fro in exactly the same manner, with the same expression, and can answer in all certainty: 'Nothing.'

12 July.

The gander hisses like a hose-pipe.

13 July.

This *Journal* can only be read by Fantec, and then, only if he has the murky soul of a man of letters; and I need to write a 'preface' for him, explaining the *letter* and the *spirit*.

1899

18 July.

The rat is on the end of the branch, the cat is on the trunk. Neither moves. A rifle shot. The rat falls. The cat jumps, sniffs the air and moves off, impressed nonetheless by her own powers.

21 July.

This life seems like a trial run.

26 July.

Man is born with his vices; he acquires his virtues.

More than once I have tried being morose for a whole day. I have not succeeded. Not even that!

The donkey who tries to weep but can only bray.

1 August.

If they built the House of Happiness, the largest room in it would be the waiting-room.

8 August.

A thunderstorm. Quick! Get to your work-table, so if you are struck down it will be on the field of battle.

6 September.

I cannot abide my plans being thwarted, above all when I am certain of never carrying them out.

23 September.

Dickens, yes, of course! But the timbre of his humour does not please my ear.

17 October.

Are we so sure, then, that we are born in order to live?

The road hugs the mountain as braces hug a shoulder.

This evening Paris seems like a vulgar farce. Pretty girls working the pavements, with all the risks involved, who would unquestionably make good marriages in the provinces.

They think of themselves as men of action, because they always take the best seats in the railway carriage.

Of all that we write, posterity will retain a page, at best. I would prefer to choose the page myself.

26 October.

I do not like Music, but I enjoy all kinds of music.

1 November.

In Hell I will be pecked to death by all the partridges I have killed.

26 November.

The tourist. In fifteen minutes of conversation he puts me off visiting half of the globe.

1 December.

You need not tell the whole truth, but you must tell nothing but the truth.

2 December.

A playwright at work on a new piece should avoid going to the theatre, or he will find in every play he watches something of his own.

8 December.

The theatre. Always tell your friend: 'You will have a huge success.' He will not bear you a grudge if you are wrong, since he's making the same mistake as you.

10 December.

When you meet a poet, it is useful to have a few of his verses by heart.

22 December.

Woman-hater – in other words, one who falls in love with the first woman he meets.

I should like to be old and able to look at a pretty woman without her thinking that I want to sleep with her.

26 December.

Cadet received a letter from an Englishwoman to whom he was once nearly married: 'I love you still, as a man; as a Frenchman, I *execrate* you.' Hard to exaggerate how many '*x*'s and '*r*'s this member of the Comédie-Française rolled into that word.

Irony does not dry up the grass; it merely burns off the weeds.

1900

2 January.

Buy a plot in perpetuity – next to the communal ditch.

4 January.

Two sisters, who are now beyond hoping that a husband might still come between them. Twenty-six and twenty-eight years old. Same hats, tied under the chin. They tell the same stories at the same time. Each contributes her own details. A sentence begun by the first is completed by the second. It is both charming and sad. Because they are poor, they are not ashamed of being unmarried. They give lessons, the older teaches music and the younger painting.

If I were rich I would marry them both. They are as fresh as unpicked cherries, but on the verge of becoming clouded and morose.

10 January.

'When I get rich,' says a child who has not enough to eat, 'I will buy myself a sandwich.'

22 January.

Maurice. Six o'clock in the evening. At the behest of Mlle Neyrat, the Society for the Protection of Animals has just sent me a Pomeranian. The children are already playing with him and have given him the name of Papillon, when an employee from the State Railways arrives to tell us that Maurice has fallen into a faint and cannot be revived. It puts me in a bad mood; death is very far from my thoughts. I think of Papa's fainting fits. I'll bring him round, give him a good shake, tell him that when you're unwell you must go to bed.

Rue de Châteaudun, No. 42. People blocking the hallway. A small, fat man, wearing his legionnaire ribbon, runs up and says, 'Your poor brother is very low.' Then, in my ear, so that Marinette will not hear: 'Dead.' The word means nothing.

'Well,' I ask, 'so where is he?'... I hear more words: 'Keep Madame occupied, don't let her go upstairs.' I ask them again, with mounting anxiety, to show me where. We climb the stairs.

Here he is, stretched out on a pale green sofa, mouth open, one knee raised, his head resting on a telephone directory, in the attitude of a man who is tired. He reminds me of my father. On the floor, water stains, a rag.

He is dead, but it will not sink in. Marinette cries a little, cannot breathe, asks where is the doctor. I pass my hand over my forehead, repeatedly, conscious that this gesture is pointless, and I ask them how it happened. He had complained several times of the heat, of stomach cramps. Just as he was leaving the office he collapsed in his chair. He was carried to the sofa. A few choking sounds, hardly death rattles. Not a word was spoken. In two or three minutes it was all over.

1900

The superintendent doctor was called and tried everything. Nothing to be done: angina.

I sit down and manage a few tears. Marinette embraces me, and I read in her eyes the fear that, a couple of years hence, it will be my turn.

All I feel is a kind of fury at death and its imbecile tricks.

I try to make out, from a distance, the advertisement printed in black on the spine of the telephone directory.

I write some telegrams on bits of paper, and have a strong suspicion that, on account of everyone watching me, I am writing badly so as to make it look as if I were trembling; because it still refuses to sink in.

We wait there. They have removed the contents of his pockets. They take me to his office, I see nothing. Steam-heated, the temperature must be 20 degrees. The steam pipe was right behind where he sat. He often said: 'They will kill me, with their heating contraption!'

The ambulance arrives. Two of them bring him down in an armchair, his head covered by a napkin. I watch him being tossed about. How big and limp he is! At the foot of the stairs they lay him out on a stretcher, then carry him to the carriage. It leaves a trail of solemnity in its wake. Death is passing, who is everyone's relative.

Rue du Rocher, he is laid on his bed. I put a handkerchief over his face.

The children cry out to Marinette, 'We love you!' and promise to behave themselves. And then there is the dog to be played with, solemnly.

I go to the police station and sign papers. In the streets, the usual evening activity. It does not sink in.

Little by little, Maurice Renard will make way for his big brother 'Félix'. Then it will sink in.

Marinette and I sit with him until four in the morning. From time to time I lift the handkerchief. I look at his slightly open mouth. He is going to breathe in. He does not breathe in.

His nose, which was a little bulbous, takes on a clearer definition. His ears harden into shells. What if he were to sit up? He does not sit up.

He is already stone. The face yellows, the features become pinched. I embrace him for the last time. My lips stick to the cold hard forehead.

His life has passed into the furniture, the slightest creak of which sends shivers through us.

23 January.

He is placed in the coffin. The plumber arrives with his little stove, then some men carrying a sack of bran, for insulation, then three coffins: one of pine (the lightest), one of zinc, one of oak. Maurice is wrapped in his winding sheet and laid down. His arms have to be uncrossed. There is no cracking sound.

How many times do I hear these words: 'He was a model employee who cannot be replaced.'

The appalling existence of the model employee!

24 January.

Ragotte tells me that she was in Pazy, when a woman who had come from Corbigny said: 'Have you heard the news?' – 'No.' – 'Monsieur Jules is dead. They're bringing him home tomorrow.' Ragotte ran back in a blind hurry; she could not walk fast enough; she said to herself: 'Such a lovely lady, Madame Jules, and always fussing over him! If only, now, it had been Monsieur Maurice instead!' When Philippe set her straight she was overcome with relief. She had carried me, dead, in her heart for three kilometres. From which I derive a certain idiotic satisfaction, as though it makes me finally interesting.

During the night of the wake I asked him several times, almost out loud, to forgive me for having been unfeeling towards him. Except that, on his side, he hadn't been too brotherly either.

The death of my father was an object lesson. If Maurice had fallen ill to begin with, perhaps – but I don't know! – I might have been of use in his final days.

25 January.

A funeral fit for a poet. I am told that his colleagues have ordered 'the most beautiful wreath' for him. The hearse is covered, the coffin placed on a ramshackle brake carriage whose horse gives the impression of having this morning been daubed in black for the purpose.

I walk behind my brother. Pierre Bertin, Borneau, Robin and others arrive. The wreaths roll this way and that. Sometimes the horse moves too quickly and then suddenly slows down.

It is cold. We walk, hats on our heads. When a group arrives in front of us, I greet them all. At the edge of the village, the mayor, wearing his sash, is waiting for me and asks me for the burial licence. He walks ahead of the carriage and leads the way to the cemetery.

Crossing the village I am bare-headed. Women on their doorsteps. A few houses with shutters drawn, where the fearful are skulking. I see left and right the fields which my brother and I have walked. It is silent, impressive. The sun shines. All is well.

The carriage, entering the cemetery, knocks against the iron railing. The corpse is lowered into the deep grave. A fat worm at the edge: looks as if it were rejoicing, doing a jig. The women start to throw down earth, some throw a pinch, others handfuls. The chink of a stone.

I move away to weep.

My sister goes to see the priest. I tell Marinette to follow her. Until the very last moment he hoped to be called upon, and had put off saying Mass until eleven o'clock. As a priest, he finds the civil interment a great misfortune for his parish; as a friend, he takes part. He hesitates before accepting a hundred-franc note. We tell him that he is not obliged to say it comes from the Renard family. He takes it.

2 *February*.

Maurice was a second impression, so to speak, of my father – not widely read, and did not remain in print. He is already being scattered in space. We must print his portrait on a separate sheet.

14 February.

Standing next to a woman, I always feel the slightly melancholic pleasure one has on a bridge, of watching the water flowing beneath.

20 *March*.

I am armour-plated, and sorrows merely rebound against me.

11 *April*.

'Do men follow you in the street?'
'Often. I am easily mistaken for a *demi-mondaine*.'
'What do they say to you?'
'Nothing of interest. Otherwise I would stop walking.'
'So what do they say?'
'"Madame, you are cruel . . . Madame, say something to me . . . Madame, may I have the pleasure of walking you home?" To which I say: "By all means, if you would like to be meet my husband." To which a labourer replied (and it was the most amusing thing I have heard): "That's a good one! No flies on her!"'

2 *May*.

Maman. Marinette talks me into going to see her. My heart beats a little faster, from unease. She is in the hallway. Immediately she starts crying. The little maid doesn't know where to look. She kisses me at length. I give her a single kiss.

She takes us into Papa's room and kisses me again, saying:
'I am so happy that you came! Maybe you'll come more often, now and then? Oh! I am so miserable, my God!'

I make no reply and go into the garden. She says:
'Yes, look at the poor garden! The chickens don't leave a blade of grass.'

I am hardly outside before she falls at Marinette's feet and thanks her for having brought me. She says:

'He is all I have left. Maurice never cared about me, though he came to see me.'

She wants to give me a silver fork and spoon. She offers Marinette a clock. One day she said to Baïe: 'At Saint-Étienne I saw such a pretty little penknife for you that I nearly bought it.'

It has been more than a year since I last saw her. I do not find her aged, so much as fat and flabby. It is still the same face, with that something odd going on behind the eyes, as in the photograph where she is holding Maurice on her knee.

No one cries or laughs as easily as she does.

I say goodbye without turning my head.

Even at my age, I swear that nobody unnerves me as she does.

2 June.

It seems that the Chitry parish priest is mortally wounded because I never returned the visit which it took him three months to decide to pay me. He does not say so: others say it for him. Every time that he and the curate of Corbigny dine chez Louis Paillard, they gossip about me.

'What did I tell you?' says the Chitry priest. 'He is ambitious, your Renard! He came to Chaumot to keep an eye on his election prospects. He is looking for advancement. Having failed with the Académie, he gets himself elected municipal councillor. He has certain illusions about the local people. I have talked to him. I know what he is: a dreamer and –' here he smiles – 'a poet. He is proud, too. He was offered the job of deputy to Monsieur de

Talon; but he was too proud, so he had Philippe named instead. I am telling you! He gives us his hired man as a deputy . . . And he wrote *Poil de Carotte* to get his own back at his mother, who is such a fine woman!'

A copy of *Poil de Carotte* is going around Chitry, annotated in more or less these words: 'Copy found by chance in a bookstore. This is a book in which the author speaks ill of his mother, to avenge himself upon her.'

On the old road, two kneeling children are stroking a pig.
'Is he sick?'
'Oh, no. He's just pretending.'
While they caress him, the pig plays at being asleep, stretches out and grunts with gratitude. His wide-open ear is as black as an oven, and the fingers of the little ones wander over his filth.

6 June.

One thinks about death, when one still hopes to escape it.

Lamartine daydreams for five minutes and then writes for an hour. With art it is the other way round.

My imagination is my memory.

I have jungle nostalgia. Just like Kipling.

12 June.

[Universal Exposition]. Belly-dancing. Obscene to begin with, and then slowly becomes fascinating. A beautiful girl, solemn expression, breasts and stomach rolling beneath a pink gauze, she is like the goddess of Turkish delight. The gauze rides up above her navel. You feel that this is truly an art, and that in the judgement of all these mesmerized crouching men some performers are mediocrities and others are divas.

The contortions of the belly are merely lewd, but the rolling of the buttocks, haunches, breasts and shoulders, and the little darting motions of the head, are very fine.

One of the girls, while dancing, lowers herself onto a bottle which she covers with her skirts, rises to her feet again with the bottle stuck (where? – in her behind, no doubt), continues dancing, crouches again and puts the bottle back in its place. Then, lying across a table, she places four or five glasses on her belly and makes them chink against each other, rhythmically, merely by the rolling of her muscles.

18 June.

There are moments when life goes too far; art must be on its guard against all exaggeration.

Baïe has learnt to do her homework, purely in order to teach her doll to do the same.

The task of the writer is to learn how to write.

At Germenay they still ring the bells to ward off a thunderstorm. How to convince them (Flammarion's *Popular Astronomy* in hand) that the bell-ringer is at risk of being struck by lightning?

They would listen to what I had to say, of course. At the next storm they would refrain from ringing, lightning would strike the bell tower, and the church would burn to the ground.

24 June.

In the British pavilion, Guitry shows me paintings by, I think, Reynolds. No need for explanations: their beauty reaches to the depths of my being. This is the art of love. Children, little girls, women, all leaving us with the sadness of not being loved by them.

'And then,' adds Guitry, 'it is achieved with the slightest of means. Through the paint you can see the grain of the canvas.'

'As for that, I could not care less.'

4 July.

'I like walking with you,' I tell Guitry, 'because passers-by say: "Look, there's Guitry" – and then they sometimes add: "And the other one is Rostand."'

5 July.

Baïe likes eating in a restaurant, because you don't have to fold your napkin.

7 July.

Paris Exposition. Chinese Theatre. A cross between puppet theatre and proper theatre. Like clowns, they beat each other and no one gets hurt, and they have expressions which would be the envy of our finest actors. The hand gestures infinitely supple.

At the aquarium. Agonies of a diver who wants to scratch his nose. Nothing excels the seahorses. They carry themselves as erect as brooches. They go up or down in the water by curling and uncurling their tails.

11 July.

The Golden Age, no – the age of gold, yes.

15 July.

I foresee quite clearly that I too will reach an age when a rifle blast to the head can no longer do me any harm.

26 July.

A sonnet. Fourteen lines in search of one idea.

27 July.

Philippe has had tears in his eyes only once in his life: he was watching the hail come down.

9 August.

Those who have spoken best about death are all dead.
To think that one day my friends will stop each other in the street thus:
'Did you hear? Poor old Jules . . .'
'Well, what about him?'
'Gone!'

11 August.

The white blackbird exists, but is so white that it cannot be seen, and the black version is merely its shadow.

16 August.

Telegram from Minister Georges Leygues to Edmond Rostand, 13 August 1900:
'M. Edmond Rostand, man of letters, 29 rue Alphonse-de-Neuville. Dear Sir, Jules Renard, whom you have strongly recommended, will be awarded his decoration. He will be among the group to be honoured on the occasion of the Paris Exposition. And you, Dear Sir, will be awarded the Légion d'Honneur tomorrow. I am pleased that the vicissitudes of life – and of political life – allow me to perform this honour, for one who does the greatest honour to French letters. Kind regards, Georges Leygues.'

8 September.

She is pretentious. Each of her words seems to have been rolled in flour.

8 October.

I describe the effect of my decoration on my family.

'Ah, one's family!' says Capus. 'My father did not even notice my decoration: as I had foreseen, he was already senile. The other day I looked at his photograph, on my table. I laughed and wept at the same time. It made a great deal of noise, which was not entirely lacking in filial piety. As for the medal, it no longer has any purpose, not even in railway stations. Everyone now has a red ribbon; they hand them out with the train tickets.'

9 October.

The medal. So many messages of congratulation, as if one had just given birth!

Our regrets, which file past in their little policeman's uniforms.

12 October.

Our vanity does not age: every compliment is a first.

Those who choose to be cremated think that, reduced to ashes, they will escape God.

15 October.

A couple.

Him: 'I ought to take advantage of my trip to Paris to buy myself a pipe.'

Her: 'Exactly. I saw some nice ones this evening. I nearly bought you one but was afraid you would scold me.'

They have been married for nearly twenty years: she has never got used to physical love. However extinguished, she still burns bright with shame. She fears his desire and his blows. Sometimes he gives her a conjugal tap on the behind which makes her cry out.

24 October.

The other day it was a coachman, at the door of the Bon Marché, this morning a 'high life tailor' who asked me for a 'deposit'.

'A what?'

'Read the sign at the cashier's desk. Everyone leaves a deposit.'

I have an urge to shove my medal in front of his nose:

'Did you somehow manage not to notice that I am a chevalier of the Légion d'Honneur? So much for bothering to seek fame and honour these days!' I merely say:

'It's all the same to me (*spoken with fury*), but let me give you my opinion: with this system you are going to lose a lot of clients.'

'Not at all, Monsieur,' replies the salesman calmly. 'It may put people off at first, but they get used to it and keep coming back.'

'But I am not carrying any money.'

'We would be happy to pay a visit to your home, sir.'
'Why not make a few enquiries?'
'It would involve too much work, sir.'

So, my name, my address, carry no weight with them. I never had to put up with this sort of annoyance before I was decorated.

Ah! pride! And the quantities of it that we lavish around us every day!

26 October.

At Corbigny they are in no hurry to serve you, and are perfectly amazed when you pay your bills.

31 October.

At bottom, the greatest actors detest fine phrases, by which I mean: what is well written. Fine sets, fine costumes, fine gestures – yes. But they couldn't care less about what they are given to say.

13 November.

Baïe, who has scarlet fever, tells the time by her little Swiss cuckoo clock. She is not quite sure how to tell the time. She knows, for example, when it is after two o'clock, or before, and if it is two o'clock exactly. She can tell the time, she says, 'when it is right'.

We buy her dolls which will only live for forty days. When she is better we will have to burn them.

The melancholy history of a doll purchased at the onset of scarlet fever. She is cosseted. Her hair is combed every morning.

She is washed twice daily. She is always propped on the bed, never left on a hard chair or on the floor. She is very contented, except that her Maman never takes her for a walk. Finally, she is overjoyed: Maman gets up, finally, makes herself beautiful, and prepares to go out. Astonishment of the doll that she too is not being got ready. Stupefaction when Maman takes her up, kisses her, murmurs 'poor little thing!' – and throws her on the fire.

18 November.

When, in the course of a day, a man has read a newspaper, written a letter, and not wronged anyone, that is more than enough.

20 November.

The little electric shock to the brain at the sight of one's name printed in a newspaper.

26 November.

Adultery.
'So the point of it is not to cause distress to one's wife?'
'As long as she does not find out.'
'But she always finds out.'
'How so?'
'No matter how – through everyone, through no one, through oneself. Listen! I leave nothing to chance, and if I cause pain to someone, I want them to know it.'

29 November.

During dessert, Baïe studies the circulation of blood in blood oranges.

17 December.

To wash your dirty linen in public – using, for soap powder, the ashes of your elders.

18 December.

Victor Hugo is so much the great man that we don't even notice that he bears the ridiculous name of Victor, just like you or me.

22 December.

The train passes, and its flock of steam tarries, so as to graze in the fields.

A horde of crows takes flight. One alone remains, through who knows what act of crow misanthropy, refusing to follow the others.

Civilized duck, murdered near the mill, by a human savage.

My father. My father. Just now, my hand on the doorhandle, I hesitate. Out of fear? No. Before opening the door, I give him time to leave the room, to which I assume he keeps coming back.

One day I shall surprise him.

Like the air itself, the dead inhabit – this is a fact – the places where we are not.

Any day now, my mother will be dead. I shall get to know another ghost.

If even a single pig were to know its destiny in advance – with that face, those teeth, such gruntings, such a head, heavy and powerful – the human species would soon get its comeuppance.

The inside of a pig is as fragrant as a bride's trousseau. What fine linen, this veil of fat that peels off!

There is nothing without its use, in a pig, except for a little sac of bile, which even the dogs won't touch.

We are the same: what we have that is least useable, perhaps, is our bitterness.

What lets the hare down are its swervings and its ruses. If only it ran straight ahead, it would be immortal.

1901

1 January.

Venice, yes, I know – at night it is almost as lit up as the Gare de Lyon.

The Philippe couple: their union is symbolized by their artless habit of eating their soup, all of their lives, out of the same bowl.

This *Journal* drains me. It is writing but not work. Just as making love every day is not love.

8 January.

We fall in love once, or twice; have one or two real friends; hate one enemy; feel pity for a few unfortunates – and the rest of mankind leaves us perfectly indifferent.

16 January.

Victor Hugo was at the centre of everything. Try to be your own everything. Stay on course at the centre of yourself. Be the Victor Hugo of your hidden and ordinary life.

It is amusing to see two young girls in the street, two sisters in full mourning, burst into uncontrollable laughter.

23 January.

I am alone in wearing my ribbon on my overcoat. Others are hardier. At the risk of catching pneumonia, they boldly open their coats so that the buttonhole of the jacket may be seen.

Yesterday, the 22nd, the anniversary of Maurice's death. I hardly gave it a thought. I have an ungrateful memory. My excuse for it is my contempt, increasingly unbridled, for all that is serious. It is all a joke.

24 January.

Raynaud asks me who is my protector, the prominent person (Anatole France? Lemaître? Rostand?) who always and everywhere speaks well of me, who gives orders, and thanks to whom one cannot open a newspaper this past year without reading 'Why are we still waiting for Renard to be decorated?' For example, who forced *Le Petit Journal* – so unversed in literary matters – to give a proper notice to *Poil de Carotte*?

Dumbfounded, I reply: 'Whatever success I have had, has been for three reasons: I merited it, I did not ask for it, and I have been helped along the way (as is always the case) by a bit of snobbery mixed in with some good fortune.'

28 January.

The two of them cling to each other as tightly as the balls of the clasp on a purse.

Frigid encounter of two medal-holders: 'What! Not you too?'

How God, who sees everything, must amuse Himself.

4 February.

I tell Tristan that when he was thirty-four, travelling incognito, Victor Hugo found his name written on the walls of churches. 'Yes – on his second visit,' says Tristan.

5 February.

After scarlet fever, whooping cough, a touch of pleurisy, what will she have next? The face of a doctor who no longer knows what to think. A persistent fever . . .

He listens to her chest. Baïe can no longer breathe properly. He thinks her liver is swollen; the pleurisy has not spread, but nor has it disappeared.

'I am not worried,' he says, 'but I can find no explanation for this state of affairs.'

Marinette and I do not look at each other – the eyes say too much. How easy to imagine the death of this small creature! The short, rapid breath that is her life. Why would it not suddenly stop?

And my boundless egotism sets me thinking: 'I have watched

my father... my brother... Must I see this too?' We are egoists. All the same, I would gladly accept an exchange of hostages, I die so that she lives. (Only when I am worked up, naturally.)

I will have lived a life of egotism, though I can tell you that it has its limits: there are moments when you leave it far behind. [...]

Eleven o'clock at night. Still forty degrees of fever, the burning little body, the small soul devoured by an inner furnace, a reflection of which flickers along her cheek. Under her closed lids, is she asleep? Are you asleep? The eyelids flutter. They alone have strength to respond.

And the mother at her side, who would give her own life drop by drop in suffering.

Next to this, what is the heart of a man of letters?

15 February.

Medicine is certain only of the idle hopes with which it then dashes us.

18 February.

The odd feeling of unease when one writes ill or speaks ill of God.

To write the complete life of Poil de Carotte, without arranging anything: the unvarnished truth. It would be the Book of Lepic. Put in everything. The embarrassment when he took me into his confidence about that young girl – pretty, and pretty sordid!

Sometimes, I imagine discovering that I am not his son; how

it would amuse me. Not to have to say that I am his son. Set it all down, with naked cynicism.

End it after his death, with a sort of hymn in his honour, done in small strokes. A book that would make you want to howl and weep. [...]

He told his first daughter: 'If you ever stop loving me, do not tell me.'

'I used to run up the stairs, so as to set eyes on her a second sooner.'

'And me?'

'You? Oh, you appeared uninvited.'

'I am not offended.' [...]

He despises me because I seem uninterested in chasing after women. His scabrous stories embarrass me more than they do him. I turn away, not to laugh, but to blush.

21 February.

Yes, it would amuse me to discover that he was a cuckold, and that I am not his issue. It would explain a great deal. But I never have such luck in life.

1 March.

I say to Guitry: 'Are you a fatalist? Are you superstitious? Do you think about God now and then, like La Bruyère?'

He replies, with a peal of laughter that could bring the house down around our heads:

'Not in the least! Ne-ver!'

At thirteen, he knew everything. The actor Monrose got him

into the Conservatoire. Signed up by the Comédie-Française. Transferred to the Gymnasium, and had to pay a forfeit of 10,000 francs for breach of contract. Thence to St Petersburg where he earned 40,000 francs and was as feted as General Boulanger, because he led a mad life, got married, got divorced. He spent more than a million and cares nothing for money.

Samuel had offered him between five and six hundred francs to play *La Veine*. At the moment of signing: 'Would you be happy with five hundred?' asks Samuel. – 'Oh, whatever you say,' replied Guitry, who felt embarrassed on my behalf.

He affects to despise what he does for a living. Nothing easier than to be a good actor. 'What I do,' he says, 'is not worth a hundred francs a day, but because circumstances have made of me someone unusual, I am paid five hundred.'

4 March.

Nothing so disgusts one with life as leafing through a medical dictionary.

14 March.

'The only sincere reviews,' says Blum, 'are anonymous reviews. That is the whole story of English journalism.'

19 March.

I cannot vouch for my taste, but my distaste is beyond all doubt.

23 March.

Love kills intelligence. The brain and the heart act upon each other in the manner of an hour-glass: one fills up, only to empty the other.

1 April.

Cousin Nanette draws her chair up close to mine.

'If someone had said to you, "Baptize your child and she will be healed," what would you have done?'

'I'd have taken this someone by the throat and thrown him downstairs.'

It was she who started it, and she keeps going until, almost in tears, she gasps: 'Enough!'

'But you are giving up on your mission,' I say. 'You must keep trying to convert me.'

She would like me to keep up appearances.

'You are ignorant and conceited,' I tell her.

'So you don't believe in Our Lord Jesus Christ, and is it not He who gave us Baptism?'

'No! It was invented by John. And that bothers you, doesn't it? You are not equal to the truth.'

'I do not have my books to hand,' she says.

'But I have them – in here,' I say, touching my forehead. 'Admit it! You have lost, as usual.'

Clumsy and pointless exchanges. She remains obstinate, and I get nowhere. But I need to refresh my irreligion from time to time.

20 April.

Léon Blum drags his blind grandmother around Italy. 'You would do just as well,' says Tristan, 'to take her on the circular railway around Paris, making sure to call out the names at each stop: "Florence", "Venice", etc.'

5 May.

We need to do for the heart what Descartes did for the mind: a clean sweep, followed by an entirely new building.

13 May.

Marivaux's *The Legacy*. The plot turns on an unspoken phrase (the 'I love you too'), which is uttered at the end, because, as the countess herself says, 'otherwise there can be no end'.

It was equally a matter of practicality to choose, as characters, a marquis, a chevalier, a countess. By their titles alone, the public knew them for what they were. Today, everyone is the same. We go to endless trouble to distinguish between each other; it is a waste of time and effort and we never get it right.

There are only a few dozen expressions in any comedy by Marivaux which sound as if they were not written today.

30 May.

The cow is going to calve, and the bull will know nothing about it.

Hawthorn. This morning the whole hedge is getting married.

Goldfinches, dressed like jockeys.

The cuckoo pronounces its *koo*s after the German fashion.

8 June.

Make an anthology of the moon.

The poet Ponge comes for lunch. From his small basket he takes out a bottle. It is a home-brew, a blend of plum and eau-de-vie, three years old. He also takes out a book which I lent him, and a poetry manuscript.

Eventually I point out that he is unbuttoned. He does up his jacket.

'No!' I say, '– your fly.'

'You're right,' he says, but there is no button.

He chooses his words with care; he says that, thanks to the grudging attitude of the householders of his village, the hedges lining the roads are in a state of 'anarchy'.

He would have liked to be decorated for services to the arts, to stir the 'emulation' of his children, but says he no longer wishes for it, having seen the likes to whom these decorations are handed out. Anti-clerical and republican, he goes to Mass sometimes in order to see his friends. [...]

He writes out his mediocre verses with their false measures, without blemishes, single-spaced, double-column, in a notebook bound in newspaper.

11 June.

The cow. Her calf was taken from her this evening, and given to Raymond, who will raise it. What will she do now, this good mother who never tired of licking her sticky offspring, no doubt more for the taste than out of maternal instinct?

When she comes back to the stable, I almost expect a scene. She sniffs the straw on which the calf has lain, and lows softly. She eats a little of the straw, which carries the taste of the calf.

Then the door to the hay-rack opens. Although she has just come from the meadow, she avidly eats the hay that Philippe gives her. She is still calling her calf, but she lets Ragotte milk her. We give her bread, which she swallows.

In two more days, she will remember nothing. Her maternal feelings, which seemed so deep, will have vanished. Already they can no longer be heard.

Marinette. At the cemetery, she sits down and, under the names already incised on the stone, inscribes all our names with a finger that leaves no mark. There is room for us all.

27 June.

Certain illnesses give an agreeable foretaste of the sweetness of death.

12 July.

Mme Lepic. Perhaps the truest thing I have done, and the best theatre, was her way of watching and hearing everything.

She will die unchanged.

As soon as I step into the garden she senses it, and sends Marguerite out to check.

If I come near the house, I hear the window creak slightly, and I know that her eye and ear are pressed against the crack.

She casts around to find something to say to me. At last, in that voice of hers, hard, shrill, and dry as gunshot, she yells out – so the whole village will know that we have spoken:

'Jules, Marinette just left. Did you run into her?'

'No!'

Alas, this leaden syllable which falls from my lips is all I can find to say to a mother who will shortly die. I walk on. She, with her face against the bars, hurt, helpless, does not draw back, or not at once. She does not close the window yet, so that the neighbours may think that we have continued talking.

How often my father felt like strangling her when she came into his room to take a towel from the cupboard. Then she would go out, and then come back in to replace the towel. He had the cupboard sealed up.

La Gloriette. What I see from my bench:

– a road; the canal, the pool and its little landing stage, wood, tiles, coal, sand;

– a road which cuts across the one that passes in front of my door;

– the river Yonne; the mill, the chateau amid its pines and poplars, the little railway, the church tower and a few of the Chitry houses;

– pastures, trees, fields, and, further along the river, the spot where I fish;

– Marigny, with its church tower, Sauvigny, with its farm nestling under the sky;

– a solitary tree in a field, a wood to the left, a wood to the right, the wooded shallows where the Yonne flows; another village, far enough away that I always forget its name;

– on the horizon the foothills, from which rises – cloven in two like pliers – the knoll of Chitry Mont-Sabot; the sky with all its cloud-fantasies;

– to the left, Chaumot school, a farm, the wooden piers of the canal, the small crosses, the Bargeot fields where I hunt, the meadows full of cattle;

– a row of little houses proud to call themselves 'Fairview'; more fields, an expanse of wheat, the birch coppices through which I can make out distant Germenay, the mound of Asnan, yet more sky . . .

26 August.

The horse, blind, walks sideways, but does not leave the metal surface of the road. He is deterred only by the sonority of the bridges: he halts, overcome by fear.

George Sand, *Impressions et Souvenirs*. To Charles Edmond, 1871: 'I do not deny it. I am naïve enough to set down, each evening, usually in a few brief lines, sometimes at greater length, the narrative of my day, and have done so for twenty years. Which does not mean that this *Journal* deserves to be published, and I have no idea if certain pages might merit publication. I leaf through it. I think it insipid for anyone other than myself.'

29 August.

When travelling, the pleasure I take in looking without seeing anything.

16 September.

When we made our first communion, he already exuded a farmyard air. In the washrooms, every morning, he washed his hair under running water. He thought it made his hair turn lighter.

To see once again a man one knew intimately twenty-one years ago!

He was affectionate, hard-working, gentle. When someone said, 'I bet I can kiss you!' he said: 'By all means.' Which was poor manners on his part: so he was not kissed.

There was no one at his first communion. I had him 'come out' with me.

He dined with the ladies Millet, who had never seen anyone eat so much.

We exchanged notes, a bit of paper folded in two with an address.

These fragile memories of childhood are a little embarrassing when one is not a poet. The poet alone refuses to blush for the time in which he said and did childish things.

But one must submit to these reunions: the taste is bitter, and it sets the limits: you can only revive the past when you are quite alone. When there are two, the harmony is gone.

How he has changed! But not at all – it is I who have changed. He has stayed still and has not moved. But what use are memories to them – they have their animals to see to.

17 September.

I hear the oysters yawn.

Thunder. You hear footsteps. Someone is moving about up there!

At table, Philippe wipes his moustache with his crust of bread.

The swallows, in their dinner jackets.

26 September.

The chestnut, that hedgehog among fruits.

My first communion friend.
More than twenty years since I last saw him. Gare d'Urzy, empty. I venture out. There is a tilbury waiting, fine-looking horse, a youngish man and his little daughter. It's him. In the carriage, I glance at him furtively: drill suit, heavy yellow shoes. Dressed for a drive. It all comes back to me, the smile and the voice of twenty years ago; it is still there, weak, muffled, rapid. I fail to catch some of his words.

We arrive in a well-kept farmyard. No one on the steps. We enter a kitchen. Is this the maid? It is his wife. Where the devil do they get these wives? Plain, self-effacing, awkward, charmless, a tuft of hair on her cheek. As he says, some run after wealth, others after beauty. He was not interested in beauty. I stand there, awkward, hat in hand. Let's go and look at the farm! I ask him questions without listening, then I ask them again. I am not as intelligent as he expected.

Lunch is served! They have removed the rush matting, whether for form's sake or for economy, and my feet rest on cold tiles. A pretty serving girl. We are told where to sit. My place is here, but I have to go and find a chair. White wine or red, chicken in mushroom sauce, radishes and butter, then pigeons in a juice so clear that they could be taken for moorhens. The little daughter looks pale, I prescribe quinine tonic and cod-liver oil.

I congratulate him on his success as a farmer. 'You like your calling?' – 'I would not trade it for all the tea in China. But I see from your buttonhole that life is treating you well too?'

He thinks I came to see him merely to show off my decoration.

He spits into his handkerchief, which is better than spitting on the floor.

I make a point of being in good spirits, and he remarks: 'I thought you would be more severe.' I think to myself: a writer is a thinker. Always thinking about something else.

I could not be more alien to him, even were I to try. My opacity is so complete that it does not bother me. Unable to interest him in my work, I try my utmost to interest myself in his work.

'So! You are a happy man.'

'Yes,' says he, 'when I work.'

He has lived for four years on this farm, with a poultry wife and a little serving girl. He could never take a break, he would die of boredom. He will eventually change this one for a less demanding farm, that is all.

'It's the same for you,' he says. 'Now you write big books. When you get older, you will write smaller ones.'

A sculpture on the dining-room table. I feel its weight, like a connoisseur. What is there to lose?

His cattle have foot-and-mouth disease. He puts one foot

between their thighs, then with the point of his knife he injects them in the back.

Not a book in sight. If there are any, he hides them well; but he was the first in the whole region to buy a harvester-binder, all the way from America.

During lunch the little girl says nothing. 'She is never usually like this,' he says. 'Ah, if you could hear how she carries on!'

No understanding of politics. 'Here, we are only interested in the bottom line.'

No book-keeping. He carries his figures in his head.

And never any question of finer feelings.

Hands and nails kept clean by work. Unattractive way of smoking, rather ostentatious, ready-rolled cigarettes.

We are utterly different, but our dogs are miraculously alike.

The wind that knows how to turn the pages, but cannot read them.

15 October.

Toulouse-Lautrec was lying on his deathbed, when his father, an old eccentric, came to visit him and began snatching at flies. Lautrec said, 'Stupid old fool!' and died.

23 October.

She is the most faithful of wives: she has never deceived any of her lovers.

28 October.

Perhaps they will say of me: 'He was a simple man of letters, who made do without electricity or telephone.'

2 November.

Julien Leclerq. Thirty-six years old. His burial, the sky almost invisible, the weather is so perfect. The gravediggers have gone about their work the wrong way. Unable to remove the ropes, they have to bring the coffin back up, out of the grave. A momentary resurrection, this brief return to the land of the living.

Loie Fuller herself, sitting opposite to me in the omnibus. A familiar sight, the thickset young woman with a mania for making herself up like an actress.

Plump fingers, shapeless, where only the rings suggest where the joints might be. She smiles periodically, as if the whole omnibus were her audience. Vague eyes. Myopic. High heels as if on stage. After all, you have to give yourself a lift in real life too.

She has no coins to pay for her ticket. Is obliged to descend at a wine-merchant's to get some change.

I have an urge to say to her: 'Mademoiselle, I know your work and am one of your greatest admirers: here are six sous.' But what would be the use.

6 November.

Fantec. Yesterday, explaining a passage of Ovid, I get exasperated, to the point of treating him like an imbecile, giving myself a sore throat and headache into the bargain. An absurd night ensues. Fantec has an upset stomach and has to get up several times. I have already started to feel guilty.

'We should not have sent him to school this morning,' I say to Marinette. I sense that she has something to say to me. She comes out with it, finally, tears in her eyes:

'I do think you shout at him too much. In his position I would also be stupefied, and it is obvious that he panics.'

When he comes home, I say:

'Your mother is of the view that I shout too much. If it paralyses you, tell me frankly. I speak to you as an equal. I want to make a man of you, and I have decided as a matter of policy to be straight and fair, and not to wield an authority that I do not think I possess. Do you find that I shout too much?'

'Uuh, no!' he replies.

'Sometimes, carried away by the desire to make you understand, I say: "You are acting like a nincompoop, like a half-wit!" Is this hurtful to you?'

'Uuh, no!'

'You use an expression – "How should I know?", or some such – which seems close to open revolt. Is it open revolt?'

'Uuh, no!'

'When I say: "You are driving me insane! I'm of a mind to hurl your books out of the window and no longer bother myself with you" – does this make you afraid?'

'Uuh, no!'

'You realize that, when I get myself into these states, it is on your account?'

'Uuh, yes!'

'If I shout, it is because I have a strong voice, and hot blood, and I wish to instil in you my ardour for study. You are not worried that I may forget myself to the point of thrashing you?'

'Uuh, no!'

'There you have it!' I say to Marinette, who is listening to us, both astonished and touched.

'Now I understand nothing,' she says to Fantec, 'so why do you not answer questions which even I could answer, who know neither Latin nor Greek?'

'Dunno,' says Fantec.

And Marinette, moved by what I have just done (addressing my son as a man, who asks for nothing more than to shoulder the blame), is more than a little vexed by him. Truly, communication between father and son is made more difficult when the father prefers not to be master of the situation – to the point of injustice. For his part, the son seems unruffled by this whole drama.

'So, your upset tummy,' I say, 'it is not I who gave it to you?'

'Uuh, no, Papa.'

'And when you bite your lip it is not because you want to cry but are holding back your tears?'

'Uuh, no, Papa!'

'It is merely a tic?'

'Yes.'

'Very well. Run along and do your homework.'

'So you see?' I say to Marinette.

'I do not understand him,' she says, chastened, 'but you I *do* understand!'

I seize the moment to tell her that sometimes I find her a little harsh with Baïe, and that, for me, the mere recollection of last winter's illness would prevent me from chastising her.

'What, me! Harsh?' says Marinette, wide-eyed. So I do not press the point.

It is perhaps the greatest lesson of Poil de Carotte, his final test. He will try, in raising his children, to do the opposite of the Lepic duo, and it will all be to no purpose: their childhood will be just as miserable as his.

At the core of Fantec is blank indifference – or perhaps this small being thinks it best to take everything that comes in good part, even my outbursts.

But will the family I made *give back* as much, in the way of literary material, as the family that made me?

The difficulty of being a man!

17 November.

Automobiles, conveyances which seem to have bolted and left their horses behind.

Keep working. No matter on what. As long as I work. Write a book of six hundred pages and call it *The Etruscans*.

How infuriating, not to be Victor Hugo!

I explain to Athis what I want: to borrow money from a publisher rather than from a businessman, and repay him with my books; and, if my books do not suffice, with my house when I sell it, or with my inheritance when I inherit it.

'Nothing is easier,' he replies, 'the only surprise is that you are not more demanding.'

The future suddenly looks rose-coloured.

Only once did Hugo let me down: when I first met him. It was at the revival of *Le Roi s'amuse*. He struck me as old and rather small, rather as one imagines the oldest members of the Institute, which must be full of these tiny old men. Later on I got to know Georges and Jeanne Hugo. I could not understand how they could worship any god other than he. [...]

I can joke about God, or about death: I could not joke about Hugo. Not a word he wrote strikes me as absurd.

I have read a few of the great thinkers: they make me laugh. They beat about the bush. I do not know if Victor Hugo is a thinker, but he produces an effect that, having read a page of him I start to think passionately, my mind wide open.

I doubt that I would ever have dared admit to him that I write. [...]

To analyse Hugo! When I look at a sunset, what do I care that it is not setting, but that the earth is turning around it? When I read Hugo, what do I care to be told that he writes like this or like that?

2 December.

Barnum's Circus. Exhausting trying to follow what is going on in three different rings.

Art is what is rare. So, if after one magnificent elephant I am shown a dozen others almost as handsome, the first will no longer astonish me.

No true artist would consent to be part of a crowd.

The monsters' booth. The most impressive: two children soldered together by their muscle tissue. Something about it that sets one dreaming.

9 December.

Yes, I wear my decoration. One must have the courage of one's weaknesses.

Old age arrives suddenly, like the snow. One morning you wake up and realize that everything is white.

Maman in her armchair, by the stove. As soon as she sees me, she goes 'Oh! Oh! Oh!' She kisses me greedily. Oh, that flabby cheek which has nothing of a mother's cheek! And immediately she starts talking at the top of her voice. When I leave, she goes with me as far as the garden gate, so that the neighbours will know that I have come to see her. She says goodbye over and over again. When I reach the cross she is still talking. I do not dare to look at her. I am always afraid of her eyes, cold, glittering and vague.

16 December.

Fantec is getting to be delightful. Sometimes I love him as though he were my father.

17 December.

With each death-notice I am sent, I amuse myself by replacing the name with my name.

Homer lived inside tragedy; it was his natural medium. Our tragedies are a sham, necessarily so.

22 December.

Andromaque. Andromaque spurns Pyrrhus, who spurns Hermione, who spurns Orestes. What a spectacle of ready-made humanity. What a wealth of love-interest! And all it needed was a poet of genius.

1902

3 January.

My public lecture on Molière, Corbigny, 29 Dec. 1901. Edgy and restless all day. I am told that, despite the rain, people are coming from Chaumot. Touched, I prepare a few words of appreciation. Through Philippe's fault I arrive three-quarters of an hour early. Nobody there. I find this comical, and the comedy of the moment restores my confidence. It is always the same story: you must try and think of something else.

I talk for an hour and a quarter without fatigue, without touching my glass of water. That ought to increase my standing! They listen to me, standing, without shifting their weight. I can make out only two or three familiar faces. At one point, I see someone yawn behind his hand. In front of me, a small girl, fearful picture of consummate stupidity.

The unfortunate audience! I get the impression that I may have overdone things; let's spare everyone and bring it to a close.

One deaf individual is listening hard, head turned to one side, hand cupped to his ear, with hideous grimacings of attention.

These people feel respect only for the person who 'cannot be fooled'. They will say about a dreadful old hag, contorted by avarice: 'You can say what you like, but she is what she is – and she's nobody's fool.'

The labourer and the peasant come to a lecture to be amused or instructed; they may or may not pass judgement afterwards. The bourgeois comes for the sole purpose of passing judgement. He rations himself, he withholds assent.

The applause is violent and short. The ladies feel that their presence alone absolves them from any further effort of concentration.

How beautiful life would seem if, instead of living it, I could watch it being lived!

13 January.

Louis Paillard arrives hot from Corbigny with the latest news. Philippe's verdict:

'They can say what they like! Not one of them could have talked for an hour and a quarter without a shot of brandy.'

The chaplain of Corbigny, a young man, seeing *Poil de Carotte* on a table, told the assembled company:

'Take my word for it! From a literary point of view, this is absolutely worthless.'

The parish priest, a decent sort, turned to Paillard:

'But you, on the other hand, wrote Monsieur Renard a very favourable notice.'

'I merely said what I thought.'

'You astonish me. Anyway, just as well to be on your guard. The man is dangerous: the ideas he has about religion!'

'He believes what he says.'

'How is that possible!'

His ancient aunt told Paillard:

'You know, your Jules Renard is not as well known as all that!'

All of them attribute political ambitions to me. They do not dare come too close, for fear of being 'tarred' by association. But they concede that I am an honest man.

14 January.

I never ask for news about those who are absent: I assume they are dead.

24 January.

Please, God, don't make me die too quickly! I shouldn't mind seeing how I die.

27 January.

Philippe's lifelong dream was to have a large blue gardener's apron, with a pocket for his secateurs. In this way, he would no longer split his trousers when he knelt down. How were we to know?

29 January.

A young man who is about to be married asks for a copy of the Marriage Code, and, after leafing through it, says: 'Divorce is covered somewhere in here, no?'

1 February.

The theatre is the place where I am most bored, and where I most enjoy being bored. Guitry can never get me out of his box.

I do not venture out into society, because I am fearful of not receiving enough compliments.

To be as autonomous as an anarchist and as holy as a saint.

From the entire life of Napoleon, I would not be able to make a play lasting five minutes.

13 February.

I realize that literature does not nourish its practitioners. Fortunately, I am not hungry.

At every moment I must grab by the throat and strangle the fox of envy, who gnaws at my entrails.

I have a horror of rhyme, especially in prose.

15 February.

Dream. In a dormitory. I in one bed, she in the next. I whisper: 'Come here!' She comes. I begin by pressing her against me, I feel under her chemise. I dare to bring my hand downwards, then upwards, moving over the soft skin, the hard breasts, as I cover her face with kisses. As I detach my lips from hers, for an instant, I see, at the foot of the bed, a prefect looking down at us, sternly and sorrowfully. She hurries back to her bed. I hide under my sheets. It is over.

18 February.

A grandfather clock, as stiff-backed and flat-chested as an old English lady.

20 February.

A little Savoyard goes into a butcher with a ten-cent violin, to buy some sausages. When he tries to pay, he realizes he has forgotten his money but offers them his violin as a pledge. A violin, of whatever water, is worth more than a couple of sous' worth of sausages, so the pledge is accepted. A few minutes later a fashionable gentleman walks in, makes his purchases, notices the violin and examines it. 'But this is a Stradivarius!' he exclaims. 'I will give you five thousand francs for it.' Astounded butcher, who then describes the provenance of the violin. 'Very well,' says the gentleman. 'The little Savoyard will be back. Buy the violin off him at any price. Then I will reappear and pay you the amount agreed.' The little Savoyard returns. The butcher gives him 500 francs, and waits for his 5,000. But the fashionable gentleman never returns.

Donnay says of Wagner's *Siegfried*: 'But these are things that one sees played out every day in real life. Why bother going to the opera!'

So long as the philosophers cannot tell me the meaning of life and death, I shall not give a fig for their notions.

28 February.

Weep! But not a single tear must reach the tip of your pen and dilute your ink.

3 March.

This evening [after visiting the Jardin des Plantes] I would say that men are less alive than beasts, and beasts less alive than the stones of Notre-Dame. At the age of thirty-eight – it has taken this long – I look at Notre-Dame, and my heart breaks.

I throw enormous lumps of bread, which the animals insult me by pecking at.

One piece lands on the back of a bear, who carries it around unawares. Success. On the ground, enormous green or yellow heaps of dung.

A barn-owl lands, feels his way with his wing like a blind man with his stick.

Geese, their beaks inside leather beaks.

Red-headed parrots, creaking like rusty chains.

Notre-Dame. For the first time in my life I examine this mass of stones. Am seized with emotion. In the zoo, the bird was alive, which seemed strange enough. Here, the stone is alive, which is utterly confounding. The gravity, the serenity of this saint, who raises two fingers in the air! And that other fine-looking saint nearby! And Saint Denis who carries his own head in his hands, rather than someone else's head!

1902

12 March.

The zoo. The boredom of all these creatures. The pleasure some of them take, boars especially, in having their backs scratched by the canes of visitors.

The marabou stork: Anatole France in morning coat.

The giraffe, with his black tongue, licks the wall or sinks his tongue into it, up to his nose.

The twittering of a group of guinea pigs from India.

The seals, fine swimmers, who dive as gracefully as men.

The caprice of the Creator who gives the flamingo a neck so long that He has to give him very long legs so that his beak is at ground level.

The eagle's beak, a masterpiece of cutlery.

28 March.

The violet – shrinking? No, not really. She is the first to flower, as if to refute any such comparison.

15 April.

Modesty is always false modesty.

The bird in the cage cannot know that it cannot fly.

Hedgehog. Gypsies are fond of it. They roast it over the fire, the bristles fall out, then it is finely chopped to make a soup.

In March the grass snake comes out of its hole, and exhausted by the effort, falls asleep in the sun, all shiny and new.

It is the bracelet of a dead woman.

The turkeycock has by now spent a long time standing on the back of the hen, who waits and is motionless. Now and then he slips – loses his balance a little, then regains it. Finally he makes up his mind and folds his tail like a fan. It is soon over. He jumps to the ground and marches around proudly, his fan reopened. The hen, who goes off in the opposite direction, settles her feathers with an air of saying: 'What a nuisance he is. A bit old for this game, surely. He'd be better off pecking at the ground. What pleasure can he be getting out of it?'

Now almost every night she counts her dead. She always gets it wrong. She forgets this one or that one: some of the dead are more dead than others.

17 April.

At the zoo. Schoolgirls trying hard to look only at the grimacing faces of the monkeys, but it is hard not to see the red backsides and the little wizened carrots. One monkey is delicately feeling the weight of her brother's carrot. No one says anything, but they make up for it – 'filthy beasts' – when one of the monkeys starts picking the other's nits and eats them along with a tuft of fur. The monkey expressions are profound and then, suddenly, empty. They have gleams of humanity, leading nowhere. Their eye dissects appearances, their mind dissects nothing at all.

The kangaroo jumps in precise and rubbery leaps, the whole

length of his alley, and, with his two front paws against his chest, seems to be saying: 'I'm really frightfully sorry, but when I have the urge I simply cannot resist.'

The porcupine tries to insert his nose into his wife's bottom, but she is having none of it, and he pricks himself on her quills. We laugh. He stops, nose to the ground, eyes lowered, annoyed, as if on the verge of saying: 'You bunch of hyenas, I'd like to see you try it.' One of his eyes is already gouged out. But what a penholder he would make! Another, excited by the spring weather, keeps going in and out of his cage, making as much noise with his quills as an American Indian with his arrows.

21 *April*.

A widow, inconsolable, to show that her grief is of the enduring variety, will select for her new husband only someone who seems half-alive.

In the theatre, tradition is such a tyrant that living actors all seem like imitations of dead originals.

27 *April*.

Francesca da Rimini, adapted for Sarah Bernhardt. Almost Shakespeare, and even more tiresome.

Aged seventy, the only role Sarah can act is the little girl.

1 May.

Fame. A reputation is made with cement, mortar and liberal quantities of vulgarity.

5 May.

To the Louvre, where Alfred Natanson wants to show me David, Velázquez, and some little Chardin still lifes: I mistake eggs for onions. Nothing here means anything to me.

As we are leaving, I see a blackbird with a yellow beak, quite alone, in an isolated patch of shade, against a background of green. Now that is painting.

7 May.

Fantec wants to be first in the queue for vaccination. He holds out his arm, bare to the shoulder; after the injection he says, 'That didn't hurt,' and faints.

Woman wearing a double chin of Russian rabbit-fur.

'I served under an adjutant,' says Guitry, 'who one day, during manoeuvres, gave us as a rendezvous "the middle of the fog".'

The truth is not always art. Art is not always the truth, but truth and art have points of contact: I seek them out.

8 May.

Father, I am forgetting you. My poor old Papa, now you are truly finished!

9 May.

Chez Charcot *fils*. His famous father died at the Hotel Settons, so Jean asked old mother Seguin, the *patronne*, to sell him the armchair in which the great man died. She demanded so much for it that he had to abandon the idea. Vallery-Radot told him that anyway he did not believe it was the actual armchair, which she had probably sold to some Englishman. As a result the son no longer feels like going to see the hotel in which his father died.

On a table a photograph of Victor Hugo, which his granddaughter says is the most lifelike of them all.

Guernsey. The harbour cannon used to be fired at midday to signal to Hugo that he should stop work. In the evening, at half past nine, another cannon blast told him to go to bed. His library in Guernsey consists exclusively of odd volumes of multi-volume works. He would read the first volume of a study of navigation, for example, and figure out the rest for himself.

11 May.

'You wrote of "the sadness of the faithful husband",' I say to Capus.

'Did I really?'

'Yes, in the *Petite Fonctionnaire* – and it was my phrase.'

'Ah! I knew it could not possibly be mine, but I did not realize it was yours.'

Pelléas et Mélisande, music by Claude Debussy. Gloomy tedium, and how to avoid laughing at the puerility of it all. The husband, pointing at his wife: 'I attach no importance to this!' Composed in *singspiel*. I keep waiting for a rhyme which never appears. And the sheer quantity of notes – meant to be the sound of the wind. I prefer the wind. Besides, it could just as well be the creaking of a barn door. The ladies say: 'I am moved: that is sufficient.' No! There is the quality of an emotion, and if I feel nothing I wager that you are feeling incorrectly.

At last! A couplet, worthy of a music-hall. Whistles and applause.

'I read a page or two of Flaubert this morning,' says Capus. 'He did not write so well, after all.'

'I know,' I say. Flaubert is not a *natural*. He is not a born writer, like Voltaire or Renan or Mme de Sévigné. His style is always a school essay, written in his best manner. He churns it out, and sometimes he misses. It is a kind of painting: sometimes the result is a daub.

24 *May*.

Death would be ideal if, from time to time, you could open one eye.

Life is short, and nonetheless we get bored.

1902

1 June.

Motorcycle racing: a black scrap-metal beast with two long tusks.

Did my father kill himself because he was afraid of dying?

People live more calmly after they have bought their plot in the cemetery. As if now they have something to hold on to, on the day of their death.

14 June.

Opera. *Die Walküre*. Tedium, cardboard and paste, with the village idiocy of a fireworks display: a provincial version of the 14th of July. Not a moment of real emotion or beauty. Only the ride of the Valkyries in the storm amused me – a rollercoaster. On top of which, they are tight-fisted with the stage-effects.

What am I to make of a work which cannot engage a sensitive individual of thirty-eight years of age? If this poetic bric-a-brac passes for beauty, what is the point in spending one's life seeking exact impressions, expressing sentiments which have the ring of truth, carefully choosing one's words! Opera has a monopoly on Beauty, by official edict. But it is a kind of fashionable café, a rendezvous of diamonds, décolletages and the deaf, trying to convince each other that they can hear.

One old gentleman complains that they are making too much noise in the wings – the storm scene is halted – and two minutes later he falls asleep. Was it all for that? I can think of nothing more self-indulgent, more degrading, than all this art snobbery.

16 June.

A lay brother is someone who seeks God unceasingly, and finds Him nowhere.

Faithfulness in this life is easy; but to die and appear before God without ever having deceived one's wife, what a humiliation!

The governor of an island like Martinique sees the earth tremble, rubs his eyes, is seized with terror. They come running to tell him there has been an earthquake and that most of the town is destroyed. 'Ah,' he replies, 'You put my mind at rest; I thought I was having a dizzy spell.'

18 June.

Fantec grins at his mother when he sees a pregnant woman, or equally when he finishes reading *Madame Bovary*. Nothing unnerves him, everything is comical. He is happy to amuse himself with all things, under the gaze of his mother.

23 June.

Death keeps 'trying us out'.

In order truly to see, we must first remove all the rococo rubbish cluttering our vision.

25 June.

Fantec does not want to get married, in case he finds himself with a wife like Mme Bovary.

When I think of all the books still left to read, I am certain of continuing happiness.

26 June.

When she wanted to remarry, as her son was now eighteen years old, she thought to ask his advice. He replied: 'On no account! I do not approve. Why marry? If you fancy him, just give yourself to him.'

She saw his family vault. She was overcome by sadness and fear. She had seen into the depths.

10 July.

Each time one is photographed, one thinks a god is being born.

12 July.
A woman was getting ready to tell a lie, as usual; but held back, because she was in mourning.

18 July.

The creation of the world is ongoing.

21 July.

I am intimately acquainted with my laziness. I could write a treatise on the subject, were it not such a monumental bore.

23 July.

The goose. Each step she takes on the damp earth, she leaves behind the image of a leaf.

The elephant with his great sabres of ivory, whose nose drags along the ground, who blows his nose on his stomach, and in between his legs.

The pelican with his beak in his apron.

2 August.

'Cuckold'. Strange that this insignificant little word has no feminine gender.

4 August.

My father. I feel remorse at not having loved him as I ought, given that I suffer from the same things from which he must have suffered.

20 August.

My sister is the proud possessor of a faith which her brother lacks.

25 August.

I can tell the exact moment when a book loses its footing and is no longer in touch with life.

27 August.

Her husband was killed in a railway accident – beneath a landslide.

Losing him was no loss.

At Clamecy, she represented herself: no need of a lawyer. She said: 'I do not ask for myself. I am simply asking for my children.' Having obtained for them what she wished, she then asked for herself, convinced as she was that her children would abandon her. The railway company gave her 600 francs.

She goes to see him in the cemetery from time to time, and says: 'I'm going to weed my darling one. He never liked grass. I have brought him a jug of flowers. He did not like flowers, but who cares.'

He came 'knocking' on her door the previous night. This morning she comes across the gravedigger.

'Did you see anything unusual in the cemetery?'

'No,' says he.

'When were you last there?'

'I just left.'

'And you noticed nothing on the grave of my poor dear departed?'

'No.'

'That is strange!' she says. 'I'll go and look for myself.'

She inspects the grave. 'Lord! The earth has been disturbed

a little, but not enough for him to get out. I must have been mistaken.'

28 August.

My father asking for the hand of Marinette on my behalf.

He has made sure to put on black gloves. He talks about everything, listens to Marinette play the piano, then says, 'Well, enough of this,' and gets to his feet.

'What about the request, Papa?' I ask, worried.

He smiles and says nothing. We know what he is thinking: 'Would it not be a little absurd at this point to start rummaging around for the right words? The fact that I've been sitting here, for the past quarter-hour, in your salon, talking to you, is this not evidence, Madame, that I am requesting your daughter's hand for my son? Is this not enough?'

All the while Mme Morneau, who had prepared a dignified reply, sat waiting.

'Well, we can consider the request made,' I say. 'Is that not so, Madame?'

'Why, yes! Why, yes!' says she, confused, and laughs.

Whereupon we all laughed, and kissed one another.

Prose is the language of happiness. 'Since we married, my dear, I haven't written a single line of verse, *hélas!*'

29 August.

To Fantec. If you agree to marry in a church, do not say, like all the others, that it is merely a chivalrous gesture, that it costs you nothing, that you sacrifice nothing by doing so, whereas your wife would be sacrificing her eternal salvation by not doing so. Remember that in a church you will promise to raise your children in the Catholic, Apostolic and Roman faith. Even to a priest, you should not promise what you have no intention of carrying out.

Do not condescend to your betrothed to the point of going along with a belief that you do not share. What is wrong for you can only be wrong for her too. She is made for the truth just as much as you are.

Do not imagine that everything can be shared – joys and sorrows – beyond the essential, which is a shared way of thinking. Otherwise you will suffer on account of your wife's religious belief, which will allow her to become almost impenetrable to you.

Get yourself a wife whose religious sense – rather than her religion as such – is akin to yours. Convert her to your way of thinking, before she converts you. A wife with whom you share the same understanding of God, which is to say the universe and your place in it. Otherwise, do not marry.

Or you will be unhappy, and you will not even understand why.

Not the least charm of the truth is that it scandalizes.

I do not write, because I have nothing to say.

I thought this was a fact, but, listening to your reproaches, I think it is perhaps a virtue.

2 September.

Philippe comes home from the fields, and Paul, his son, from the railways, at the end of the day. They come by the same road, but do not wait for each other. The first does not slow down; the second catches him up if he wishes.

I look at the stars. To learn their names I light a candle, and consult an astronomical atlas. But when the candle goes out, my eyes dazzled, I can no longer find in the sky the star whose name I have just learnt.

Lies are their hereditary trait. They devote themselves to lying well: in which respect they are superior.

3 September.

They have a few ideas, rare and isolated as beans planted in the ground. You need a mattock to get them out.

As soon as a truth is longer than five sentences, it becomes a novel.
It is a fine thing, a good novel. By no means contemptible, but the unvarnished truth sends one into raptures.

4 September.

Philippe does not like to dream; it exhausts him as much as harvesting.
He roots up the potatoes – in a manner of speaking, since a

light nudge with a pick unearths them. He throws them back between his legs. There is a trail of them behind him: you could almost say that he creates them himself.

After killing animals and killing each other, without doubt the most sadistic pastime of the peasant is chopping down trees.

Walks. The canal all the way to Marigny, then from Marigny to the Germenay road, returning to Chaumot along this road. With Marinette and two dogs who are at peace with each other.

A mower is scything the grass border. He says hello. Despite his courtesy, we pass him with a slight anxiety in our legs, as if the scythe might creep up from behind and bite us.

When we both overtake a waggon or cart on the same side, the men look at my decoration and then at Marinette. When she passes on one side and I on the other they forsake me to devote their attention to her, wearing a slightly low-cut dress.

A woman goes back into her house, the better to watch us from behind her raised curtain. So someone still lives in this poor old house! And it has been lived in for centuries. For what purpose?

I pass by. I take note. Some Renan or other will read this, and will join it to the life of the world. He will insert it into the universe. Their lives were lived for that reason. In *L'Avenir de la Science*, Renan writes: 'Think of the numberless generations crammed into country churchyards. Dead, dead for ever? No! They live on, as part of humanity. These dead went into the making of Brittany –' or Marigny, or the Nivernais. – 'And when Brittany is no longer, France will persist, and when France is no longer, Humanity will persist . . . On that day the humblest peasant, who needs to take but two steps from his cabin to his tomb, will live on, like us, in this universal name of humanity.'

Yes, but how to convey this to Honorine, whose arms are so hardened by poverty and labour that they are like old branches? And are we to believe that God created all these wretches of the earth for the intelligent appreciation of Renan? It seems a high price. Is this not a somewhat insignificant final cause?

A man drives his cows ahead of him, as we pass, and talks to them, from the instinctive need we have to show others that we are endowed with speech, and to attract the attention of an unfamiliar woman. Children shout and play in a meadow. Little girls press their faces to a fence.

In and around Germenay, it is like the end of the world. Meadows and woods of a blackened green, not a church tower, not a soul, not a cow in sight. Yet it is here that the sun chooses to set.

I can find only one intelligible motive for remaining in Paris: money. What of glory? Or the thirst for activity? Is it possible to find greater riches than on this road to Germenay? For this *expanded* moment, no need to spend a hundred sous to take your pleasure. A hundred sous here means bread, means the wherewithal to clothe one of these wretches, who, without knowing it, contribute to the creation of God.

6 September.

A great poet need only employ the traditional forms. We can leave it to lesser poets to worry themselves with making reckless gestures.

16 September.

The roofer. His speciality is to stop on the ladder and surprise through the window a young woman getting dressed.

A roof studded with new tiles. The sun plays draughts with them.

26 September.

Open your eyes. What I see is Chaumot and Chitry. This year, I can almost see Marigny. Next year I must try to take in Germenay. If I comprehend this corner of the world entirely – as a photograph *comprehends* every detail of the view taken – I shall not have wasted my life.

17 October.

Forain brings into the Figaro a drawing, reduced to essentials.
'All the same,' says Rodays, 'for three hundred francs, you might have put in a little more!'
'More what?'
'Don't ask me. Some cross-hatching, maybe?'

1 November.

The parish priest told him, 'Increase and multiply,' so he took no further precautions. 'Fortunately,' says his wife, 'I had a miscarriage, and put a stop to all of that. Otherwise he'd have filled the house with children.'

28 November.

Vallotton very keen on the navy, in the manner of a Swiss admiral.

1 December.

He got so bored in the country that he ended by seducing his maid. After which she took to sighing deeply while serving him at table. When he returned to Paris he forgot all about her. But she wrote:

'Monsieur has changed. Monsieur should not worry, if he has good intentions towards me. There are not many as capable as I of hiding their feelings.'

22 December.

Jaurès. Has somewhat the air of a companionable bear. A short neck, just enough to tie the little necktie of a country schoolboy. Lively expression, restless eyes. Many forty-five-year-old fathers resemble him – you know the sort, those papas whose eldest daughters take them to task familiarly: 'Do up your frock-coat, Pa.' 'Papa, you're going to have to pull your socks up, I can tell you.' [...]

What he says does not always interest me. He says the right things, and is right to say them, but perhaps I know them already, or am no longer sufficiently in touch with the people – and then, suddenly, a really fine turn of phrase:

'When we set out our doctrine, they object that it is not practical; they no longer say it is not just.'

Or again:

'The proletarian will not forget humanity, for the proletarian carries humanity in himself. He possesses nothing, except his title as Man. With him and within him, it is the title of Man that will triumph.' [. . .]

He is sustained by a grand and irrefutable conviction, which is the spinal cord of all that he says. Example: 'The progress of human justice is not the result of blind forces, but of conscious effort, of an ever higher idea, towards an ever more elevated ideal.'

26 December.

We watch smoke rising with a tender emotion, as if, at the foot of the chimney, a woman, still young but abandoned, were burning her love letters after re-reading them.

31 December.

A year, a slice cut out of time, and yet time remains whole.

1903

13 January.

A new circus. Warm stable smell. A few flies circling my head.

A clown who keeps being knocked down has a new way of falling, while trying to stay upright like the rest of us. His arms flail at the air and find nothing. A clown with talent, an original.

To introduce his sketches, he carries a little gate made of rough wood, and makes his entrances through this little gate which he places in the centre of the ring. He enters by lifting the catch; he even wipes his feet on the threshold. When he has finished his sketch, he leaves by the same little gate, closes it carefully, carries it off with him.

17 January.

Realism, Idealism, so many mists through which a blind man seeks the truth.

In my church, there is no vaulted roof between me and Heaven.

20 January.

Lamartine is a great poet who probably wrote fewer than twenty perfect lines.

25 January.

A woman laughing so much that her make-up disintegrates. Her natural colour reappears, and we see that she is a beauty.

Guitry tells a good story. He is utterly fearless. When he lies, it is not his nose that gets longer: it's mine.

Young girls are not allowed to read everything, but they may pass their afternoons at the zoo, looking at the monkeys.

1 March.

Dull weather, wind and rain. One imagines an isolated chateau in which an entire family sits yawning, saying: 'If only it were still the season for manoeuvres. A few officers might appear.'

2 March.

The woman who shows her breasts and thinks she is offering her heart.

Husband, wife, priest: the real *ménage à trois*.

When you rejoice over being young, and remark to yourself on how well you feel, that is age talking.

3 March.

The waiter brings me an empty bowl of mouthwash by mistake. I do not call him back; when he comes for it, imagine his astonishment! He had of course heard that these provincial types drink it up, but he did not believe it. I am his first.

This is all I retain from that particular dinner.

16 March.

Irony is one ingredient of happiness.

21 March.

Jealous by nature, he never invites bachelors to dinner. If by mischance there is a bachelor among the party, he changes the place settings so as to be next to his wife.

27 March.

'The world is poorly ordered,' says Capus, 'because God created it by himself. He should have consulted a few friends – one on the first day, another on the fifth, another on the seventh, and the world would have been perfect.'

30 March.

The success of others disconcerts me, but far less so when it is unmerited.

The sudden naturalism of an actor who, during a rehearsal, interrupts his flow to speak to the prompter.

1 April.

Geese. Hearty cooks who arrive carrying their little shopping bags under their stomachs.

10 May.

Theatre. Ignore those friends or members of the press who find some passages dull. They have seen so many plays that they have an urge to say: 'Keep it moving!' The public on the other hand are more likely to say: 'Slow down! Not so fast! I have paid for an entire evening, and you keep wanting to show me the door.'

16 May.

The left hand must not know what rings are bestowed on the right hand.

The fall of woman. Nothing broken: hardly a rip.

29 May.

Each time I see the word 'Jules' in print, not followed by the word 'Renard', I feel a pang.

5 July.

July evening. The brilliance of Venus, which appears after the sun goes down, and draws the bats. They are intoxicated, at every instant dropping through the air as though down a hole, without ever touching the bottom.

On the canal a bargeman, whose boat is at a standstill for lack of work, is playing the accordion. Their heads just above the surface of the water, the frogs accompany him as best they can; no use his wife telling the dog 'Will you shut up!', the dog continues barking to the best of his ability. Even a cow moos, once. The rats join in, whistling from the sides of their mouths. But all of this music cannot disturb the calm of the evening. A light breeze bends only the tops of the tallest grass.

The wall of the mill is bleached by the reflection of a full moon.

The heart is cradled and at rest.

The man of letters sometimes tells himself, as if coming out of a dream: 'But hang on! I have no occupation! I absolutely must make up my mind and acquire one.'

12 July.

The ladybird: a small tortoise which suddenly takes to the air.

1903

14 July.

The ignorance of the peasant is a combination of what he does not know and what he thinks he knows. [...]

They like their poetry rough, like the local red wine which is almost black.

They no longer know where they stand. They have lost their priest but have yet to find their sage.

They are afraid of seeming too modest, rather than too proud, because they think modesty belongs to brute creation, and they do not wish to pass for brutes.

They believe in God. They may suspect that the priest is not good, but God is infinite goodness. They gloat over the fact that the priest calls on God to strike them down, but that He does nothing of the kind.

They are waiting for someone to open their eyes and tell them: 'You are not brutes, whatever your priests may claim.'

They have made a bouquet for me, but forgot to give it to me. By way of amends, they would like to place it on my father's grave. At first I say yes, then feel a bit awkward, and dissuade them, on the grounds that my father was against demonstrative gestures – but in reality because it bores me to cross the village, under the eye of the priest, with a bouquet and a dozen peasants trailing behind me, en route to the cemetery. [...]

Reading seems to them about as pointless as hygiene, given that they are never ill. [...]

They believe in Purgatory, after a fashion: as a kind of waiting-room in which they will sit until the train for Paradise arrives.

The women are a little ashamed of their priest, whose rudeness and coarseness offends them; but they are also afraid of him.

This priest might well be the devil in disguise. But they are not certain of anything any longer, and, poor distracted souls, they keep going back to him.

At times a deeply impressive natural solemnity: they are worthy of having Homer read to them. They like me to discuss politics with them, religion too. They are ready for a lay catechism. They believe in God the same way as Victor Hugo does.

Because I have lilies in my garden I am taken for a royalist.

Philippe and Ragotte live as if during the time of the Gospels.
A tureen on a little table, not a drop of stock in the soup; followed by a head of garlic, and water to drink: wine gives Ragotte dropsy.
We look around for their tent. The camels cannot be far away.
Garlic gives them an appetite to eat more bread.

As a ranger Robert has never prosecuted anyone, and has never had occasion to, because whenever anyone wants to steal some wood, they ask him first. He says: 'Yes, but do it neatly, so no one can tell.'

Nature is never unnatural. Look how easily the trees breathe!

22 July.

'My hair is falling out,' says Robert. 'My lice have nothing to hold on to any longer.'
When he comes across deer horns, he sends them to me so I can make knife handles out of them.

White cattle, as immobile as the linen spread out on the hedges to dry.

23 July.

Mme Lepic. An actress who over-acts, hardly knowing any longer what she is doing, or saying; her one remaining thought and purpose in life: to be on stage every minute of the day. [...]

Philippe, who used to think she was kind, understands at last the kind of life my father led. He adds, speaking to Marinette: 'I refuse her offer of a glass of wine or her shot of brandy – though you know, Madame, I would never refuse yours.'

She keeps giving things away, as ever. At first it was out of charity, then it was out of pride. Now it is out of humility, so as to be tolerated, because she is afraid of being left alone.

When I pass by her house, I hear her voice, high-pitched and metallic, a voice without nuance. She is talking all by herself, to make me believe – for she has seen me, she was on the lookout for me – that she has visitors, that she is not neglected.

And she plays the great lady: she wears flounces on her sleeves, which enrages Cousin Nanette.

It is a myth, those peasant weddings, when they eat for an entire day. In effect, they eat little, but they eat slowly. To eat a lot, you must have the well-lined stomach of the rich.

One of those moments of despair when I write: 'I love no one! I care nothing for my wife, my children!' It is painful, having to write it down. Too bad, write it down! Is it my fault? Did I give birth to myself?

24 July.

They are talking about the moon again. They say:

'There is a new moon tomorrow. The weather will change.'

If you press them a little on the subject, they pretend not to believe it themselves, but say that their father, or some old village crone, firmly believed it.

Hard moon, tender moon, russet moon.

25 July.

I imagine to myself that I am very old, and condemned to entertain only the thoughts of a wise dotard.

Happy people have no right to optimism: it is an insult to misfortune.

The bull bellows behind the hedge. The cows approach, under the oak tree. One of them is dancing, as if crazed.

A bull can cover a cow from the age of one year; by the age of five or six he is already too heavy or too ill-tempered. His career is over.

27 July.

When Philippe manages to catch a mole, he takes his revenge. He turns a cloche upside down, embeds it in the earth, with some water, and throws the mole inside. Not quite enough water to drown the mole – who keeps trying to climb the glass walls, only to keep falling back into the water.

30 July.

The man who is both happy and an optimist is an imbecile.

Who has not seen God has seen nothing.

1 August.

They look at the cemetery too much, at death itself not enough.

At the Marigny school, Marinette distributes afternoon snacks. The little ones do not dare to touch their brioches. One of them is so exhausted he falls asleep.

My visit is included in the school register. The mayor tells the children that one day they will understand that I write books, just like those in the school library – where all I can see on the shelves is Jules Verne.

18 August.

This morning, leading the cow to pasture, Ragotte hears the sound of cries, loud sobbings! She runs and finds in the field a little boy guarding Bouquin's sheep. He was weeping with tedium, because since Midsummer's Day he has been hired out to Bouquin as a diminutive shepherd. He is twelve years old. He is homesick for his parents, who live in Mouron, and he starts crying again, fat tears rolling down his cheeks.

19 August.

Fantec photographed him with his dog. The wife thought there was too much husband in the photograph, and not enough dog.

'You know that the earth turns?'
'So they say.'

Tolerate my intolerance.

2 September.

The priest treats his congregation as cattle, as donkeys, as degenerate alcoholics. He interrupts the Mass to ask a little girl a catechism question. Confused, she does not answer. She will not be taking her first communion this year.

3 September.

I would not want to say that I believe or do not believe in the immortality of the soul, but it sometimes happens, of an evening, on a bench, that I think of my dead as if they were all present and correct.

A young Englishwoman, from London, leaves this suicide note: 'I am going to kill myself. Papa's dinner is on the stove.'

14 September.

You can comb the shops in Corbigny without finding a nail file or a toothbrush, and the only sponges are for sponging carriages.

Religion is their excuse for lazy thinking. You give them an explanation for the universe, ready-made and third-rate. They take care not to find any other, first of all because they are incapable of looking, secondly because it is all the same to them.

There is nothing more contemptibly pragmatic than religion.

You say I am an atheist, because we do not look for God in the same manner; or, rather, you think that *you* have found Him. Congratulations. I am still looking for Him. I will be looking for Him in ten years, in twenty years, if He grants me the time. I fear that I will not find Him: I will keep looking nonetheless, assuming He exists. Perhaps He will appreciate my efforts. And, on your account, perhaps He will take pity on your beatific confidence, your indolent and half-witted belief in Him.

26 September.

Are there wise men out there who feel for nature as I do, who find that this suffices, that there is no need to turn it into literature?

'As for me,' says Borneau, 'I have no religion, but I respect that of others. Religion is sacred, after all.'

Why this privilege, this immunity? A believer is a man or woman who believes what is said by a priest but cannot believe what is said by a Renan or a Victor Hugo. What is so sacred about this choice? What difference is there between such a believer and the fool who prefers magazine literature to great poetry?

A believer creates God in his own image; if he is ugly, his God will be ugly, morally speaking. And why should moral ugliness be respectable? The religion of a fool cannot protect him from our contempt or our mockery.

Let us be intolerant for our own sakes!

May the herd of our ideas line up behind the solemn shepherd called Reason! Let us be rid of the bad poetry of Humanity!

The beauty of literature. I lose a cow. I write up her death, and this earns me enough to buy another cow.

28 September.

Ragotte was very ill, last winter, for the first time in her life. She does not know what was wrong with her. She ministered to herself, by drinking two litres of hot water. She could not get up. She was hot all over, except in her back, which you could not have kept warm 'even by putting a house on top of it'. She coughed and coughed! At last, she vomited blood: it did not frighten her; in fact, it was what made her better.

Philippe, who was also sick, could not help her. But one evening, Paul, looking at her, said:

'I'm going to make you a broth.'

He went over to Bouquin's and bought an old hen. He quickly plucked and cleaned it, and made a pot of bouillon. It was inedible. It was filthy, Ragotte admits, but she drank every drop so as not to hurt Paul's feelings.

Ragotte has big, delicate emotions.
Her ideal: to pay what you owe and then to owe nothing.
Ragotte is the very last peasant.

A tree that stands on tiptoe, amidst the others, to see above and beyond the wood.

The leaves hold out their tongues to the rain.

7 October.

Pastorals. The biggest day of their lives: they played cards from one in the afternoon to six in the morning, and, to relax, they farted like gods.

When Ragotte married, her father-in-law wanted to give her something: a chain, or a cross or a Holy Spirit medal, a sort of silver host surrounded by rays. She wanted nothing.
She had three dresses. She never bought another. She bought herself camisoles, of course, but never a dress.
Wedded in clogs, she only became acquainted with shoes later on, when she went to the weddings of others.

Large melting pills of hail.

The Batavian lettuce rises like a Chinese pagoda.

9 October.

The mystery of the world bewilders us. But think of the bewilderment of the thrush, sitting on its branch, who suddenly gets a blast of lead in the chest!

10 October.

Him: 'I need to experience an affair of the heart before I can write my masterpiece.'
Her: 'In which case, my dear, write away: you are a cuckold!'

Death is poorly arranged. What we need is for our dead to come when we call them, from time to time, and chat with us for a quarter of an hour. There are so many things we did not say to them when they were here.

13 October.

Ragotte married in the month of October. She had just finished a season of harvesting, at twenty francs a month. She saved them up for her marriage.

'As you can imagine,' she said, 'I would have had the upper hand with such a sum! But my father took it all,' she added with resignation.

'How did he do that?'

'Oh, he simply went and found the farmer, and told him: "I have come for the sixty francs you owe my daughter for the harvest."'

'And he never gave you a sou?'

'I got married with nothing but my own two arms.'

18 October.

Forty years old, and I am too timid to go to the Moulin Rouge alone.

I would like once more to be as diligent and well-behaved as a small boy. Perhaps I still have time to be a good student, and come to a good end. Everything would need to be redone, from the beginning.

2 November.

They congratulate me for not writing too much. Soon they will congratulate me for not writing at all.

21 November.

Guitry says: 'Come. I have something of interest to show you.' He opens the door. Before me stands 'Little Tich' in person.

He has seven fingers on his right hand, two of which are joined together.

He tries to keep his hands in his pockets, but there are always some fingers poking out.

His features are both young and old, with wrinkles and childish dimples. I do not know whether to address him as 'old man' or as 'little one'.

The tiny mouth looks as if added at the last moment, when it was noticed that without it he could not eat.

The solemn demeanour of a diplomat from Lilliput.

Married to a pretty Spanish brunette. Has a son, just like everyone else.

He dislikes comedy, detests music-hall, and only reads serious books.

I am afraid to offer him my hand in case I might walk off with some of his fingers, but his handshake is firm and his 'Pleased to meet you' is loud and clear.

23 November.

The provincial bourgeoisie. They like to dine wearing black gloves.

They say: 'But, Monsieur, the capitalist also runs risks!'

They excuse themselves for going to Mass, on the grounds that they only go for the music.

Chaumot. Since we are speaking of the *Encyclopédie*, I remark: 'They have given me an entry.' No one asks to see it.

A little later, as if by chance, I open the volume to the letter 'R', and show it to Firmin. He reads the article aloud. They listen. No one says anything.

'And now,' I say, 'let us see if we can find an entry for the parish priest of Chitry?'

They laugh, saying: 'Fat chance.'

'Good,' say I. 'For as long as this dictionary exists, I too exist.'

We move on to other topics.

5 December.

I hate work, but I love my study.

We must read Bourget to kill off the inner Bourget we all carry around inside us.

Not even enough flaws to be interesting.

Christianity: a heresy of the Jewish religion.

20 December.

'I have finished my comedy for the Théâtre-Français,' says Capus. 'It only remains for me to add a few of those fine phrases which ensure that a play will never fall out of the repertoire.'

30 December.

Maman coughs all the time, not because she needs to, but to let us know she is there.
She is fond enough of Marinette, but at bottom is a little piqued that Marinette is not afraid of her.
It amazes me that when I was twelve I did not already know how to lead her by the nose. [...]
She has her charm, a species of charm to which I am immune. [...]
She is afraid of dying suddenly. She wants neither a slow illness nor a quick death.
She wants to have the time to say what she has to say.
She wants to keep on talking!

1904

2 January.

Maman can spend hours chatting with a little girl, or with a cat: purring is all she needs by way of response.

What would suit her is a kitchen giving onto the stairs, so that she could open the door and see whoever is going up. [...]

She does not lie: she invents. She invents everything, with meaningless facility, even her dreams.

You could not say that she steals: she moves things around. She pockets a thimble that she knows someone is looking for. She does not give it up immediately: she lets you hunt for it.

They are not the thefts of a grown-up: they are the tiny thefts of a magpie. [...]

Maman says that it was she who introduced boot polish to Chitry. Before that, people blacked their shoes with soot from the bottom of the cooking pot. [...]

'I am like all old people,' she tells us. 'I no longer have any appetite.' And she proceeds to drink a bowl of coffee with hot milk, and is the only one of us to eat her entire roll. She catches herself doing this: 'It's not appetite, it's just for the taste.' [...]

She says 'My daughter', but refers to Maurice or me as 'these gentlemen'.

She remembers insignificant details from the past, but has quite forgotten that she lost her first daughter. My father wanted to kill himself.

If the word 'cemetery' does not enter her head, she has no memory that her 'dear departed' are resting there.

4 January.

Her envy of Marinette's contentment, her rage against this woman who manages to be happy with a man whom everyone finds intolerable. [...]

Maman is on the point of leaving – because Marinette is happy. She tells her: 'No wonder you're happy, with the sort of disposition you have!' and starts to cry.

She writes to everyone in Chitry that she has been properly received, but is not feeling well and is coming home. She is preparing herself to say that we didn't want to let her go.

6 January.

We hear her weeping in bed. 'I had a lovely week, and now it's all over!' We are about to feel sorry for her, but then we notice that only her mouth is crying.

'I'll go upstairs and say goodbye to Jules.'

'Don't trouble yourself,' says Marinette, 'he is coming down.'

At the foot of the stairs: 'Goodbye, dearest Jules, and thank you. Farewell!'

She presses my hand, she kisses me on the left temple, through her veil. She really does quaver tearfully. I have not said a word.

It may be the last time that she kisses me ... and that I fail to kiss her. My mother!

11 January.

To write with the tip of your heart.

13 January.

Ibsen's *Doll's House*. What a deal of trivial stuff, delivered as if to seem profound! Nora's bolt for freedom probably merits just a good spanking. A play in which things are straightened out as abruptly as they are turned upside down. An affair of forgery that ends in a discussion. The only man, this bank employee who wants to hang on to his little job. All of which, somehow, despite being too long and ill-constructed and arbitrary, is not boring. It makes a change from our endless adulteries.

15 January.

In the most complete friendship there is always a little empty space, like the space in an egg.

Joy is not a pleasant sensation. A state beyond feeling. It is as though your heart were turned to whipped cream.

21 January.

The hundred-footed centipede has only twenty feet – I counted them.

1904

28 January.

Scene. A husband, through excessive zeal for the truth, driven to extremes because his wife suspects nothing, ends by telling her that he has been unfaithful to her.

30 January.

Funerals have their good side: they reconcile families.

3 February.

'Bravo!' – we don't even have the word for it in French.

'I envy your life,' says Coolus. 'You have only one passion, literature, and only one wife to love: your own.'

15 February.

The anti-Semite:
'Imagine the following. A Jew comes to you to buy some paintings. The price is agreed. The paintings are dispatched. On receiving them, he says: "I want a discount of three per cent."'
'Shame on him!' she replies.
'Imagine, Madame, another Jew who owes you two thousand francs and simply refuses to repay you.'
'The scoundrel!' she replies.
'Yes,' I say, 'but my Jew happens to be a Catholic.' And I remind her of the words of Sarah: 'I am waiting for the Christians to be better than us.'

'You like Jews?' she asks.

'I endeavour to like all men who are honourable and intelligent.'

The first fine days. A fragrance in the air like *omelette aux fines herbes*.

Outing to Versailles in Guitry's new automobile.

During all of which I feel like Richard the Lionheart. I observe passers-by with contempt; I do not even condescend to notice them – I am a man absorbed by weighty matters; or else I adopt the air of a jaded habitué.

And then I think: you poor imbecile, and it is not even your automobile!

22 *February*.

Forty years old! For the sage, death is perhaps merely the passage from one day to the next. He dies, as others turn forty.

2 *March*.

The pig, what an admirable animal. The only thing he does not know is how to make his own sausages.

Leda and the swan? No more improbable than the Virgin Mary.

21 *March*.

A chimney which the smoke leaves only lingeringly, with regret.

1904

1 April.

After serving two days in prison, for whatever reason, he is not allowed to vote: he is as happy as a man who has placed himself beyond the reach of the law.

If vegetables could read, they would be more responsive than this Good Friday crowd.

A village like Chaumot or Chitry is the finest proof that the universe makes no sense.

2 April.

Elections. An ugly interval. You hardly dare to step outdoors, or say good morning, or shake a hand – you might be soliciting a vote. Every smile is taken for an entreaty.

The voter believes himself master of the situation. There's some confusion here. But no, my good fellow! You vote in order to do right by yourself, not by me. It is I who am doing you a favour. It is you who are obliged to me.

The priest tells them a pack of lies, and promises them the moon in Paradise.
The mayor thinks of nothing but his sash.
The teacher could, if he would ...
So which one of them is going to look into the face of the peasant and say: 'You have been asleep for centuries. Wake up!'

8 April.

Philippe points at one of my big dictionaries: 'If I were forced to read the whole of that before going to bed I would definitely be out of sorts!'

16 April.

Egotism. To bring everything back to yourself. Even God.

18 April.

Nothing softens the heart of a father more than the charm of a small daughter who is just a little under the weather.

Jarry and his rifle. The bullets falling on the other side of the wall.
'You are going to kill our children!'
'We'll make you some more, Madame.'

19 April.

It is all the same to me, if I make a mess of my life. I do not take aim. I shoot into the air, at the clouds.

Never have I felt so incapable of achieving anything.

I think it will end in suicide. For already, whenever I feel a little tired of life, it amuses me, the black thought of it, and then imagining the act itself.

I was not made for the struggle. I was made for killing people by shooting them in the backside.

18 May.

Maman says: 'The most beautiful day of my life: 15 May 1904, when my son was elected mayor of Chitry.'

Village hall. The sheer quantity of paperwork, on the subject of wet-nurses! Impossible to get by without a secretary. No mayor would have time even to read the stuff.

The elections. Maybe I was the only one who took it all seriously.

28 May.

As mayor, I am responsible for the upkeep of the rural roads. As poet, I would prefer to see them neglected.

8 June.

Maman is regressing to a little girl again. She likes to be scolded, and she wails in the voice of a child who has barely learnt how to speak.

In Paris I tell them all my election and town-hall stories. To which they say: 'And we thought you were going to tell us something amusing!'

Telegraph without wires. All well and good, but I ask myself where our graceful swallows will perch?

11 June.

As mayor I am sent endless leaflets for fireworks. Do they think we do nothing but celebrate?

Branch of a cherry tree, as voluptuous as the arm of a woman.

15 June.

Five little schoolboys, playing in the dust.
In their satchels, the first carries bread and hard cheese for himself and his brother; another has bread and an egg in a little tin pot, for himself and his brother; the fifth, the oldest, has a piece of brioche, the leftover from a comrade's first communion, and a few cherries. They all drink from the well.
The right enjoyed by the head of the family to see his children starve. Almost all the peasants drink wine, almost all of them eat a hearty stew at noon; their children make do with hard cheese.

2 July.

Demolder asks a young bookshop assistant in Holland:
'Do you have *Poil de Carotte*?'
She replies, indignant: 'If my mother were here you would not talk to me like that!' It is true that she had red hair.

Broom, the radiant flower of this dark Breton soil. Gold set in coal. A facile combination, but it works every time. Not too sophisticated, 'But someone had to think of it,' God would say.

Automobile. Fields, villages, towns are reeled in, as if by invisible strings that we are pulling.

6 August.

We have to listen to Maman talking about 'sin'. 'I had my faults, I still have my faults, but I have always been able to walk with my head held high.' Perhaps. But a cuckolded Papa might have been a happier man.

'Molière, La Fontaine, old-fashioned guys like Papa,' says Fantec.

10 August.

Ah, disgust at life! But things are already looking up when, coming upon us in this state, the woman we love starts to cry.

13 August.

Maman. A great actress, to whom life handed only bit parts. Bent over in the garden, she catches sight of us and remains bent while she prepares her litany of woes.

14 August.

The visiting Marquis taps the belly of a pregnant woman and says:

'Good work! I'm also a breeder: seven children.'

He writes in his letter of thanks: 'Hand in hand, we will work towards the same end. It is my life's dream to be among you, because this is the only excuse for the rich in a modern world.'

Now there's a fine sentiment. Onwards and upwards! So much the better, if the rich start to give something back!

However, no sooner is he elected than our Marquis begins to show his true colours.

He wants to donate 300 francs to the Corbigny music *concours*, but only on condition that his name appears alongside the prizes for which his money has paid. He gives, but he does not want to lose.

Freedom of conscience means not paying the priest when you do not go to Mass.

20 August.

An old woman is trying to heave a big bundle of hay onto her shoulder with a pitchfork. She cannot manage it. She calls to Philippe.

'You'll kill yourself,' says he.

'So much the better.'

Philippe lets this pass; and she does not press her point. He raises the pitchfork for her.

'Wait till I catch my breath,' she says, wavering.

She lays her handkerchief between her shoulder and the handle of the pitchfork. She is no longer visible. The hay has taken the place of the old woman, and moves off.

From their burrows, the rabbits watch the passage – where are you, Shakespeare! – of this walking haystack.

1904

30 August.

Even the desire to kill seems to have left me.

A quail, its wings spread over its half-dozen young.

Philippe trembles when he points out a hare in its burrow. I am too close. A little further over. There.

The morning of the hunt. The moon was on our left. I loaded my rifle by its light. The sun rose, steadied itself, drinking up the moon's vapour bath.

Woman. The voluptuous way she had of pushing a drawer shut with her behind.

Papa spent the best part of his later years killing wasps.

1 September.

The lark rises. It comes to rest on a clod of earth a little further on.

It is dangerous to carry a gun. You think it doesn't kill. I shoot, not in order to kill, but to see what will happen. Then I approach. It is lying on its front, its claws clutch, its beak opens and closes: the tiny scissors are cutting through blood.

Lark, may you become the best of my thoughts, and the dearest of my regrets!

It died so that others might live.

I have torn up my hunting permit and hung my shotgun from a nail on the wall.

6 September.

The Chaumot poacher. One of the few locals who does not greet me. He is proud because he has no permit and his wife drinks. She often collapses, from destitution. He must be a socialist. He knows from experience that one is fed in prison.

What is socialism, then? A society in which everyone would be a poacher, like him, without merit: he has no use for merit.

You sense that he would dispatch you very efficiently. And if you came back to life, what a great play you could write about it!

The peasant. A simple man. Examine him, take your time, and, after two weeks, three weeks, ten years, write a page about this man: in all you say about him, there will probably not be a word of truth.

11 September.

Municipal council meeting. Tempestuous.

With regard to paying forest rangers, which I understand as little about as anyone present, I say:

'It is the law. They must be paid.'

At which Gautier, the riverkeeper – we did not grow up together – with his cavernous voice:

'You misunderstand the regulations.'

'Have you read them?'

'Good God, no!'

'Well I have, and I'm telling you: It's the law.'

I become irritated; things take a turn for the worse.

On the subject of schools, Gateau says – and it falls from his mouth like dung from a cow, as though he were pouring out his soul:

'Well, I for one don't need a school: I don't have children.'

This is so outrageous that voices of protest are raised on all sides. [. . .]

The subject of hygiene comes up. Page, who has a head like a hive of little red worms, says:

'Manure heaps never harmed anyone. Cesspools are another matter. Besides, there is no illness here. There is no typhoid fever. The animals drink from ponds as black as slurry: they come to no harm. So why would it be harmful for us? It's not manure, it's the fertilizers that are poisoning everything.'

They do not believe in prevention, only in cure.

19 September.

Honorine no longer uses sheets: she goes to sleep fully dressed on her bed.

She tries to get up on a chair to rewind her old clock. Which is of no use to her, because she is deaf, and can no longer raise her head to see the time, but likes to watch the pendulum 'tingling'. It keeps her company.

Marinette winds the clock for her and says:

'What time?'

'Make it six o'clock.'

'But it isn't even four!'

'Never mind! Make it six anyway. It makes no difference: it strikes all the same.'

One's native land is the sum of all the walks one can take on foot around one's village.

Stars: this fireworks display that has stayed hanging in the air!

Truth. A few novelists manage to coax her out of the well, but then they immediately wrap her in blankets.

Since the day I got to know my first peasant, any rural writing, even my own, has seemed a lie.

24 September.

Though I am not a practising socialist, I am convinced that this is for me the true path, the road not taken. Not through ignorance, but weakness. My wife, our children, our bourgeois background, my attitudes of a man for whom art is still, despite everything, a craft. I lack the courage to break these bonds. If I do not covet the 300,000 francs in royalties earned by Capus, I do nevertheless want to earn 10,000 francs, or 15,000. If I care nothing for the Académie, I nonetheless aspire to a certain success. If I mock society, I still have two or three friends who are Parisians, with whom I like to spend a couple of evenings a week. If I am incapable of doing what is required to shine in their world, I am equally incapable of embracing fully the alternative. So there you have it!

Envy is not a noble sentiment, but nor is hypocrisy, and I ask myself what is to be gained by replacing one with the other.

Envy – openly admitted – is a form of courage, is almost its own excuse.

Advice to hunters: go out one evening without your gun and walk through your killing fields. The magpie becomes a familiar. The partridges sit still until you are up close. The sloes are waiting to be picked, and the juicy little wild pear.

The fields go to sleep under a light mist.

The ox stops to look around, and the ox who follows licks his hindquarters with a lazy tongue.

The meadow draws to itself the entire green blanket. And no murder has been committed: that at least is something.

27 *September*.

Doctors. Always imperious, even when they are saying: 'Ah! But that is where our knowledge ends.'

Team: two oxen, four wheels connected by a wooden shaft and two cross-beams. Seated behind his oxen, the man sings. A primitive. An earthly king returning to his village kingdom.

5 *October*.

First frost. A little ice on a cabbage leaf.

Poetry. A coffee grinder operated by wind-power.

One day a week I believe in human progress, and call for it with all my might; the other six days, I rest.

11 October.

A cow so thin that her skin is stretched across her frame like a sheet pegged out to dry.

15 October.

Beetroot with a hairdo like a Red Indian chief.

21 October.

At the *Salon d'automne*. Works by Carrière, Renoir, Cézanne, Lautrec.

Carrière good, if a little too artful.

Majesty amidst vice: Lautrec.

Cézanne: barbarity. There are many celebrated daubers to be admired before throwing your lot in with this carpenter of colour.

Renoir perhaps the best of the bunch – not before time. At last, someone who is unafraid to paint: he plants an entire garden on a straw hat; at first you are dazzled. Look more closely, and the mouths of his little girls begin to smile, and with what subtlety! ... and those eyes that open like flowers! They make mine open likewise.

Vallotton. The petty dreariness of an upholsterer.

Cézanne – this is the life, all of it spent in a village in the Midi. He did not even come to his autumn *exposition*. He would dearly like to be given a ribbon.

That is all they want, these poor old painters who have led irreproachable lives, and now, near death, are watching the art dealers getting rich on their work.

22 October.

Guitry tells lies, but what do I care? I don't look for truth in Guitry, I have it in myself.

24 October.

Feminism means no longer counting on Prince Charming.

Automobiles. Never has luxury been so insolent. It is Capital, running over everything in its path, beyond reach: what murderous thefts have taken place, all to be squandered on such gross recreations.

Some of them look like engines of war. We are returning to the dark ages, of chariots fitted with scythes.

13 November.

'You are so modest!'
'Yes, but think what it costs me!'

23 November.

At the *mairie*, 19–20 November. A wedding. The flag with no flagpole. I nearly address the bride as 'Madame' when asking her to be seated. The ill grace of secretary Huot, his astonished reaction to the opening words of my little speech. The ladies weep. Signatures. Neither the father nor the mother know how to sign their names. The bride lifts her veil. I kiss her and, forewarned by Philippe, give her twenty francs for her first-born. Am invited to lunch. 'We'll come and fetch you in the carriage.' But since the early hours of the morning, consequent upon the cold weather and a broth which I ate too hastily, I can only think of vomiting.

29 November.

Guitry does not respond. Our friendship is over. Strange as it seems, I feel lighter. Perhaps this man, to whom I owe such delightful moments, was quite harmful to my inner barbarian, the worker that I am.

The memory of his friendship is no small thing, and will be more painful to renounce than the friendship itself.

He gave me more than I gave back.

He was the rich friend. Dinners, automobiles, travel, theatre, money, wit, so many stories! . . . I owe him a great deal – and what does he owe me? Next to nothing.

I am neither rich nor brilliant. Perhaps he owes me this: simply that everyone was surprised by my friendship for him. I served him as a foil, in my plainness. Without my presence, he will perhaps sink in the estimation of those who have a high moral opinion of themselves.

Even superior spirits like Guitry always end by tiring of the 'honest' friend, and by despising anyone who accepts everything they offer.

Shakespeare. King Lear a madman whose madness starts with stupidity. It is too stereotyped, like some lurid piece of folk art. The excess too calculated.

15 December.

Ah, yes! To be a socialist and make lots of money.

16 December.

Now I know what distinguishes men from beasts: money troubles.

1905

1 January.

The poet Ponge says:
'Some people tell me I'd be better off if someone were to set me up with a tobacconist's shop, rather than being given academic honours. I would prefer the honour, for my children's sake. I could not keep a tobacconist's going, because my work in the fields would prevent it; and if it had to be kept up by someone else, the profit would no longer be worth the effort involved.'

[Ragotte and Philippe.] Their mania for concealing the fact that they are ill. Their ignorance in the face of illness. Apart from 'My back hurts, I can't sleep, I can't eat,' they know nothing.

Philippe wants a civil burial. 'Would you like a few words to be spoken over the grave?' – 'Do as you like! I shan't reply.'

A cow needs to be fed in stages, three times; otherwise it will use the hay for bedding. Unlike a horse.

7 January.

Coolus relates that D'Annunzio, the first time he called on Sarah Bernhardt, stopped a few paces from her and intoned, like one possessed:

'Beautiful! – Magnificent! – *D'Annunzian!*'

After which he said: 'Bonjour, Madame.'

Moments when, I do not know why, I have an urge to punish myself.

9 January.

Jaurès says that Sylveton had no interest in killing himself; but on closer examination . . . Yes, if we look hard enough, we discover that we all have an interest of some sort in killing ourselves.

To be a socialist with your head costs nothing, but let your heart enter into the equation and you are ruined. The rational socialist can have all the defects of the rich man: the emotional socialist must have all the virtues of the poor man.

Today you can come to socialism after having been successful, after you have proved your talent – as formerly you could enter the Trappist order.

When I think that perhaps I might not be a socialist today, had I only been capable of writing a three-act play!

12 January.

In the theatre, Baïe would like to play the maid-servant roles: all you have to do is hand around the biscuits.

13 January.

Why do actors always say: 'And what might this be?' when you bring them a card or letter, instead of examining it and opening it?

Women to whom you pay a compliment, and are then obliged to take it away again.

16 January.

Rostand had a coachman, of whom he was very solicitous. When he dined, after the theatre, the thought of the coachman seated outside in the cold and rain, until midnight or later, was intolerable to him. It spoilt his pleasure. So he would have a hot toddy brought out to him, with instructions to go home and that he, Rostand, would hail a carriage.

One night the coachman came into the restaurant and informed 'Monsieur' that he was leaving his service. He was offended that he was not being taken seriously.

24 January.

A protestant: someone who stops in the middle of the road even when the coast is clear.

I have an anti-clerical mind and the heart of a monk.

26 January.

After a lengthy monologue in which I explain the meaning of life to him, to which he listens very closely, so that it brings tears to his eyes, Fantec says, with the stout voice of a big lad:
'I am going out, Papa, and I will be right back with your glue pot.'
The glue pot I had asked him for the previous day.

29 January.

Because she is the same height as me, Baïe says that now she can read everything I have written.

31 January.

At the Louvre I purchase a crown of 'bay' for the poet Ponge, while taking good care to display the fact that I am myself a chevalier of the Légion d'Honneur.

The beauty of the stock pot. A carrot, a turnip, an onion, a clove inserted like a nail into the onion, a head of garlic, a bay leaf, a leek with its strings attached, a stick of celery.
'Yes,' says Marinette proudly, 'and all of it seething away, just like the hubble-bubble of government.'

13 February.

The poet Ponge, who barely acknowledges my silver palm – he thinks I can fill my pockets with them at the ministry – says to me:

'Now all I need is the tobacconist's.'

I do not know who put such a thing into his head. A shop on which the rent would be several hundred francs. Disgusted, I lose my patience and tell him not to count on me.

They had to amputate her leg. As she has a thirty-year plot in the cemetery, for her father-in-law, she had the limb deposited there.

She has one leg in the grave.

1 March.

Schwob's funeral. Why do men of letters – before they go – not write down the speeches they would like to have read over their graves? It would take five minutes out of their lives. [. . .]

Schwob is lowered into a temporary tomb. He goes down, down, down into the nether world.

'Walk part of the way with me. It would please me greatly, but I entreat you to put your hats back on if you fear catching cold. If it is a nice day, leave your umbrellas behind. As for wreaths? Well, if you must, but let them be of the laurel variety.

'Next, spare me those long faces that make you so very unattractive. Take care that you don't start to look like me!

'Next, please do not start claiming that I united in one person every possible quality! You know perfectly well, better than I do, that it is not true. Above all, do not say I was good-natured. Being good-natured is not a virtue: it is the worst of vices, and you know perfectly well how I detested bores. Those of you who are capable of tears may shed them, but let everyone else smile and make jokes!'

2 March.

I spend my days like an old man. I read the papers a little, read a passage from this or that book, set down a few thoughts, keep warm – and, much of the time, doze.

7 March.

Schwob: 'Don't say I was thirty-eight: I was thirty-nine. And now I am ageless. [...]

'And don't say I was always good-humoured! My nature did not allow of such banalities.

'On a clean page, write down a few things about me – which is always an amusing task – but make sure it's not dull, and that were I alive I could read it without ridicule. A little wit, even a little malice would not spoil the party.'

9 March.

Barracks. Ordinary houses are not guarded: a concierge suffices; but in front of those that are full of soldiers, a sentry is posted.

15 March.

Yes, the work of Death is interesting, but too repetitive.

What the sun can do with an old threadbare wall.

A day lost in dreaming about work, and putting it off from

hour to hour. A few notes, a good find or two, perhaps. All trimmings and no substance.

I envy Marinette: she has made a soup for everyone.

I have made nothing. If only I had driven in a few nails, split some wood, sowed some carrots, written – no matter what – a few lines that would appear in print tomorrow and from which I would earn a few sous! I would not have done nothing, I would not have wasted the day.

In order to write, you clear away the obligations in your life. No visits, no meals outside, no fencing practice, no walks. Now you can work, produce something worthwhile. And, onto the wide grey sheet of the day, your mind projects – nothing.

I abolished at a stroke so many things that were important to me: poetry, fencing, fishing, hunting, swimming. When will I abolish prose? And literature? And life itself?

29 March.

Duse in *La Dame aux Camélias*. In the darkness of the theatre, some are fidgeting, others are asleep.

This actress is a single harmonious composition, truly. For the entire first act she caresses the audience. She has a way of exerting her charms on the cushions, of burying her head in a pillow! . . .

But she is none too pleased. She finds the public cold, the box-office receipts insufficient, the curtain calls too few.

30 March.

I saw fifty plays last winter. Not one of which I wished I had written.

April.

La Gloriette. 7–11 April.

Nature is not so much green as verdigris. The leaves of the horse-chestnuts are unfurling.

The tender green, too sparse, of the thinly planted wheatfields, the dark green of lucerne, the pale spray of the blackthorn.

Violets, pansies. The earth is pensive: its thoughts are multi-coloured.

20 April.

Honorine does not go to church, because she once worked as a maid for a lady who had two priests to supper – they wore civilian clothes, swore and drank, and spoke only of their mistresses.

21 April.

André playing poker at Alfred's house, whose father, stretched on a divan, lets out a resounding fart.

André starts laughing.

'Shush! You'll offend my father, and it is the only pleasure he has left.'

At which André laughs even more loudly, saying:

'It is the voice of my own father I heard.'

Maman says to me:

'You look terrible! Here are your Easter eggs.'

If she were not stopped (but she will be stopped), she would come to La Gloriette every day. When a day goes by without news she becomes frantic with worry.

She invariably says the wrong thing: to those who think they are ill, that they look fine; to those who think they are well, that they look ill.

I shall never get used to her. I shall never get accustomed to my own mother.

She brings me a dozen Easter eggs, and impresses upon Marinette that nobody else must have any of them – not the maid, not Philippe, not even Fantec and Baïe. She wants me to eat them all. Twelve hard-boiled eggs: she wants me to choke.

Out walking, we come across some cows. One of which lets fall an impressive quantity of green dung. We laugh, by way of acknowledgement, but the old peasant who is leading them says to the cow – out of politeness, because we are present – 'Dirty slut!'

22 April.

Man should be considered from the point of view of the naturalist, not the romantic psychologist. Man is an animal that can barely be said to think.

Maman no longer says, 'My son,' but 'Monsieur le maire'. Very soon she will start addressing me as *vous*, like a curate's mother.

28 April.

Seventeen years of marriage! Marinette was reluctant, but it has been what is best in my life.

3 May.

How difficult it is to be good! I hope I never succeed.

Maupassant. He was too often satisfied with plausibility.

23 May.

Maman asks can she darn my old socks, as though it were an honour.

30 May.

There is no need to despise the rich. It is enough not to envy them.

I take little excursions into my interior, on my lake of ennui. Joyous little excursions.

1 June.

Marinette is afraid I shall lose my sense of involvement. I tell her that vulgar ambition must not be confused with zest for life.

'With you,' she says, 'it always comes out right. I am not afraid of the bull in the field. With one motion, you shoo him away from us.'

'I used to be afraid of death,' I tell her, 'but today I can smile when I picture myself lying in my coffin. I used to be afraid of storms: I no longer give them a thought. I still fear suffering, but not dying – the thrust of the sword, but not being killed in the duel. The essential is not to lose you; as for the rest . . . I don't chase after most things, but I hold fast to the main thing. I was once afraid of certain ideas: I am no longer afraid of any idea. I admit everything, except causing the person you love to suffer; or causing anyone suffering, for that matter. You stopped me from becoming a satirical poet; I am an elegiac poet instead. I keep within me a fund of naïveté that is like eternal youth. I defy whatever is fine and alive and elemental not to move me.'

9 June.

They reek of servitude still. The fire is lit in the chateau, the shutters of the dining-room are opened, the count arrives. Smiles all round, and bowed shoulders, and already the hats are coming off the heads.

As it is the patron saint's day, I told the watchman to do his rounds this evening and not to spare the drunks. The first one he encounters is his father.

17 June.

We rescue an ant with a twig of straw, and if it falls over again we call it an ingrate.

21 June.

I remember the special odour I noticed at the time of my father's death. It comes back to me every year, at the same season. I shall end by believing that it is the smell of death.

I discover it is the odour of roses that have wilted in their vase.

My father died in June, season of roses.

Bent by the wind, the bulrushes salute me gently with their swords.

26 June.

Read several pages of Stendhal on the city of Bourges, in *Mémoires d'un touriste*. Perhaps I should blush for my ignorance. Stendhal's account amuses me, but during my year as a volunteer in Bourges I did not once step inside the cathedral. As for the palace of Jacques Coeur, I must have passed its façade with quickened pace many times on my way to catch the Paris train. Nonetheless, I have no wish to re-do my year of military service.

Stendhal says that on his arrival in Bourges he felt stifled by an atmosphere of bourgeois pettiness. I did not experience even this.

28 June.

The piglets never get confused, beneath the stomach of the sow, and each of them knows, from the first day, which of the teats is his.

July.

On Indolence. A book I must write! The fool who recognizes his folly is no longer quite such a fool, but an indolent individual can be aware of his indolence, bemoan it, and remain indolent.

In Clamecy, a prim little village, everyone pees against a corner of the town hall. No corrugated pissoirs for privacy – so that the bourgeois, whose windows all give onto the square, by lifting a corner of their curtains, can tell from behind which citizen is now peeing against the wall.

5 July.

Maman exclaims: 'Ten metres of fabric! Oh, my dear, it is too much, a thousand times too much! Nine metres would have been quite enough.'

I warn you that the worker sweats, smokes, spits, picks his nose, and pares his nails with a knife. You will notice none of this, out of delicacy, but do you have the stamina to stay the course?

The affecting life of a tree, that throws itself desperately about, as if trying to take a step.

19 July.

As slow as an old woman climbing the stairs with a telegram for you.

27 July.

Wilde in his *De Profundis* makes us regret not being in prison.

31 July.

The lightning strike of 28 July, at three in the morning.
Borneau is recovering. He laughs, proud of having survived a lightning bolt, proud too of having almost been killed.

'I got down on all fours,' he says 'and scampered into the street.'
Deafening, the tearing noise of the thunderclap.
'Don't be afraid!' I said to Baïe.
Lucienne calls Philippe, her father. Through the doorway I see Chitry on fire. We get dressed. Lantern (to ward off the lightning flashes). People at their doors, in the street. Men coming out of their houses.

'It's at Borneau's place!' they say.
'How is Borneau?'
'He was rescued, but Mougneaude wanted to go back in to get her quilt, and has not come out.'

Ah. And the pumps? No water. Shouts. Ladders. The men forming a chain.

It is now daylight. My lantern, which I carry from place to place, must look ridiculous. [...]

Mougneaude on her bed, old, insensible, almost extinguished.

'Take off her nightgown! Cut it open, cut it open! Does that help? Rub her with wool, get warm water – no, cold water.'

A spoon between her teeth. I search for the tongue, I pinch it, impossible to get hold of it. Handkerchief. Movement of her arms. The green of her teeth. The white body of an old lady.

She'll come through.

The priest arrives, puts on his white surplice, reads his prayers and opens his phial of oil to administer extreme unction. I do not take off my hat, but go outside.

While we try to revive her, he is busy burying her.

Honorine says that what threw her was a bolt of lightning out of the sky.

In times of distress the peasant wants to rise to the occasion. Borneau wails like a professional mourner.

The hens ran out of his hen house, on fire.

8 August.

On the 6th, prize-giving at Châtillon-en-Bazois. [...]
'We know Poil de Carotte better than you do yourself,' says the schoolmaster.

'Indeed! He has taken my place.'

'You invented him for that reason.'

The only real compliment the book has received.

9 August.

Pointed church spires, built on prominences. Excess of confidence in God, chastised by lightning bolts.

14 August.

Vézelay, deep impression – except for the Benedictine abbey; I rejoice that it says nothing to me. But what a past! This great dynasty of monks ...

18 August.

Socialism must start in the head and descend to the heart.

Here, only the barn doors preserve for a while the evidence of political debate. Candidates and voters are soon forgotten.

25 August.

Ragotte does not know how to wash things in a tub. She goes on a hike when she has even a rag to wash, to soak it in the river, in the running water.

Going to Mass and washing in the river – ancient and sacred customs.

Their daughter died on Sunday and was buried on Tuesday. During all of Monday he threshed. Nor did she give any sign of a woman who has lost a daughter: rather the air of one who has four cows to milk, twice a day, morning and evening.

When do they have time to grieve?

3 September.

Fantec tells me:

'I said to Montagnon, in Nevers, hoping to get an invitation to his pottery works: "I am Jules Renard's son." Montagnon said: "But of course! the pharmacist at Clamecy!" – "No!" – "But of course, the captain!" – "No!" – "But of course, the naval lieutenant!" – "No, the man of letters." – "But of course, the one who wrote little novelettes and made quite a success of it."'

1 October.

Hunting with hounds and shooting, all of it is contemptible and without excuse. One does not hunt to feed oneself. The only excusable hunter, were any of it excusable, is the poacher. At least he sells what he kills and lives off it all year round.

'But you kill chickens, you kill cattle!'

'That has nothing to do with hunting. Neither the chicken nor the cow are at any point aware of death. They do not fear us. They have lived well, thanks to us; their death is almost the payment of a debt. Between the life of a chicken and that of a partridge, no sane animal would hesitate.

'Observe, in the first days of October, how the partridges flee headlong in all directions, panic-stricken. Their life, which they have had so much trouble in defending against hail and drought, and beasts of prey, now becomes a thing of abject terror as soon as men appear with their sticks that create noise and smoke. And then take a look at the contented chicken you will eat tomorrow!'

The peasant is perhaps the only specimen of humanity that does not enjoy the countryside and never pays it any attention.

4 October.

Maman is sorrowful; a real sorrow which, though it will not last, is affecting.

She is beginning to suspect that paying each other visits is not the solution to every problem.

A picture of melancholy: an old woman, her chair balancing on two legs, crouched over a fire consisting of two smoking logs. Behind her, the cold of the kitchen.

She finds in her son the same silent man that was her husband; what is more, the husband is invisible, as ever.

To wait on her, she has Lucie, a little maid who wears mourning and moreover seems never to be there.

She is losing the strength that made her talk incessantly. Her words fall into the fire, and others do not follow. There are long silences.

She weeps and says:

'Oh, I have so much grief! Can you not see how much grief?'

Heredia the poet has died. He leaves behind only a single volume of verse. He must have thought himself home and dry: 'Surely posterity cannot refuse entry to one slim volume.'

But it is as easy for posterity to ignore one as to ignore a thousand.

10 October.

Old age does not exist. At least, we do not suffer continuously from being old; like the trees, we have, each year, an attack of old age. We lose our leaves, our good humour, our zest for life; then they come back again.

We do not have childhood followed by maturity followed by old age: we have our seasons, in cycles; but their course is not well known: it is not clearly laid out.

11 October.

Sheep being minded by a youngster so small that the wolf might easily gobble him up when they're not looking.

18 October.

Out hunting. Two hedgehogs in their leafy nest. Pointu nudges them out of the hedge with his paw, like chestnuts that are too hot to hold, then takes them in his mouth – but they burn, so he lets them drop to the ground.

23 October.

Maman. Solitary, brooding by a meagre fire while behind her the wind blows through the cracks in the door and the holes in the window.

She has one amusement left: to find fault with her maid, whom she sends out to work by the day for all the neighbours.

Each time she fastens on one or other defect in the girl, she is sure to add:

'You see, I am quite the opposite. You are young, vain, and untidy. I am old, no longer vain (thank God!), and I am clean. And you are hard-hearted. Yesterday, you put away all your late father's things, his tools, his overalls, his jackets, his trowel, without so much as a tear in your eye. Me, I can't stop crying just to think of you having to do such a thing. At table, you have no manners, you help yourself before me. I would never have dared help myself before the rest of my family.'

Maman does not care for the idea of being reunited with her loved ones – in their unconsecrated free-thinkers' graves.

'Oh, the common grave! That will be good enough for me!'

'Don't talk nonsense,' replies Marinette. 'You know very well that you have your own plot.'

But her secret, unconfessed hope is that her plot may chance to be next to that of the countess.

I care no more for the immortality of my name than the immortality of my soul. If I could arrange things with God, I'd ask Him to turn me into a tree – a tree which, from the height of the Croisettes, would look down on my village. Yes, I should prefer that to a statue.

25 October.

Only time itself does not waste time.

1 November.

The little ones greet me as I pass.
'Good day, little ones!'
I walk on, and behind me, despite the respect I am owed, one of them farts and they all burst out laughing.
Was it deliberate? That is not the issue.

3 November.

Life is not so long! Not long enough to forget the dead.

5 November.

Life is badly ordered. The ignorant poor should be rich, and the intelligent should be poor.

6 November.

Return to Paris. Dejection. Were it not for Marinette, I would escape by the ten o'clock train. Marinette's chronic indecision about Paris.
'Back there we are kings,' she says. 'Here, the concierges are as well provided for as us.'
The dining-room feels small. The house is poorly constructed. The floor creaks under my foot. It is disturbing, and absurd: to have comfort, fresh air and a happy life back there, then to come and spend six months in this furnished boarding house!

1905

15 November.

It is not hard to be a socialist; what is hard is to resign yourself to not having a penny.

Socialism: sanctified envy.

28 November.

At Chitry, an old woman dies. Her son, who let her go without bread, provides her with a plot in perpetuity. The bread is forgotten, and everyone says: 'What a good son.'

1 December.

Suicide. No thought of the tomb, or the horrors of death, but a boundless wish to blend in with the irresistible melancholy of things.

3 December.

Things seen. An old man running behind a tram, catches hold, lets go and tumbles to the ground. The conductor stops the tram. The old man gets to his feet and boards the tram. The conductor reprimands him: 'It is forbidden ... The company declines to take responsibility ...' and so on. Added to which, a well-turned-out gentleman, on the viewing platform says to him:

'You have hurt yourself.'

'No, not at all.'

'But yes, you have! You must have injured your left elbow,

where it is torn, not to mention the right one! You feel nothing now, but you'll feel it later. Tonight it will take hold, and you won't be able to sleep. Tomorrow you will ache all over. You'll need to call the doctor.'

By now the old fellow, thoroughly ashamed of himself, would almost prefer to be under the wheels of the tram.

8 December.

Omnibus. The unscrupulousness of those matrons who do everything to force their way inside, before their turn, gives some idea of how they will behave at the gates of Paradise.

12 December.

Paris is getting to be fantastical. These buses without horses... We all seem to be living in the Underworld. And the thought comes back to me: 'Are we not all dead without knowing it?' Through this noise, these shadows, this mist, you walk with anguish, less from the fear of being run over than the fear of no longer being alive.

Impression of an immense cave, and your brain turned to pulp by the roar.

22 December.

He lost a leg in 1870: he is keeping the other one for the next war.

1906

Chaumot, 3–7 January.

The priest distributed a circular to find out who would like religion to be kept up. Those in favour were treated to a boiled dinner by the count.

24 January.

Posterity! Why should people be less stupid tomorrow than they are today?

26 January.

The truest, most exact word, the word most filled with sense: 'Nothing'.

I can credit whatever you say, but the justice of this world does not reassure me as to the justice of the next. I fear that God will just carry on blundering: He'll welcome the wicked into Heaven, and boot the good down into Hell.

The cat who sleeps twenty hours out of twenty-four is perhaps God's most successful creation.

Yes, God exists, but knows no more about it than we do. [...]

I do not know if He exists, but it would be better for His reputation if He did not.

30 January.

Only today do I see Paris for what it is.

Twenty years ago I could not look. I had only my ambition. I only read books.

Now I stop in front of the Louvre, in front of a church, at a street corner, and I say to myself: 'What marvels!'

What was I thinking about before my eyes were opened?

From now on I am going to admire everything about you: your monuments, the pink clouds of your setting suns, the cocks and hens on your quays.

1 February.

In the shadow of a famous man there is always a woman who suffers.

9 February.

Philippe's ears: two apricot halves eaten away by wasps.

10 February.

Imagine his wonder, today, were Man to come across a rose for the first time! He would not know what wonderful name to give it.

12 February.

The religion of superior beings: desire for discipline. They have no faith: they believe because they need to believe. It is the taste for prison, and I often have it myself.

13 February.

To the socialists: 'Yes, by all means, let's share resources! But let us also share loyalty, courtesy, and wit!'

22 February.

Forty-two years old. What have I done? Next to nothing, and now I do nothing at all.

I have less talent, money, health, fewer readers, fewer friends, but more resignation.

Death appears to me as a wide lake that I am approaching, whose outlines I begin to make out.

Am I any better a person? Not much. I have less energy to do wrong.

Of my forty-two years, eighteen spent with Marinette. I have become incapable of doing her any ill, but am I capable of the effort it takes to do her any good?

I miss the time when Fantec and Baïe were so small and so comical. What will become of them? Am I as concerned as I ought to be?

I sometimes think of my father, seldom of Maurice, they have both been gone a long time. My mother still going. How will I manage to pass from her life to her death, paying proper attention?

To get up in the morning, work, attend to others, it exhausts me.

The good things in life I still do pretty well: sleep, eat, daydream.

I am also good at envying others, running them down.

I don't seem to get any better in argument: I shout as loud as ever, though less often.

Indifferent to women, on the whole. Here and there, a whiff of romance.

I hardly ever read new books. I only enjoy re-reading.

And where do I stand on the question of renown? Since I shall never have it, I can scorn it without too much effort. I am almost sincere in this, though I say so too often.

25 February.

Little Paulette Allais has been put in the care of a serving woman, who tells her that her dead father is surely in Hell by now, and the little one wakes at night crying out: 'Papa is burning! Papa is burning!'

27 February.

Bigots communicate with the Virgin Mary by special telephone.

Theft, less hateful than lies.

I taste the bitter joy of splendid isolation.

Clouds with an air of having been thought up by poets.

1 March.

A pair of misers, who play a piece for four hands on the same piano.

5 March.

Marinette has only ever refused me one thing: the right to sit and dream in the falling dusk. Remorselessly, she says:
'Time for the lamps?'
I dare not demur, and she brings the hateful lamp, which puts to flight all my thoughts.

Life is short, but is drawn out by boredom. No life is too short for boredom to find its niche in it.

Flaubert had little time for nature, but missed it when he was away from it.

10 March.

Académie Goncourt. Yes, I accept – as long as I do not have to compliment all my colleagues on their talent.

13 March.

Make a summary of my notes, year by year, to show what I was. Write: 'I liked this, I read that, I thought such and such.' Which goes to show – no progress.

Imagine life without death. Every day you would try to kill yourself out of despair.

Poetic injustice.

I re-read my notes. Whatever else I might have done, life could not have been much more eventful. What more I might have produced – good and bad – would not have added much to the sum of my works. My works!

There are names which no longer mean anything to me. I cannot recover the features of certain faces, forever buried.

Were I to begin again, I would want the same life. I would only open my eyes a little wider. I have not looked properly, have not seen all that was there to see, in that little universe in which I was feeling my way.

What if I were to try and work again, regularly, every day, like a student of rhetoric who wants to be first in his class – not in order to make more money, not to become famous, but in order to leave something, a little book, a page, a few sentences? For I am not at peace.

Earn your living, but not to excess.

Do not try to eat twice as much, so that your neighbour will have half as much to eat.

Do not say, 'I alone am the voice of reason,' but try to reason nonetheless.

Take from the various moralities what is worth taking, and from Christianity what is good. Jesus Christ was a modest and estimable individual, after all: He was not one to shout 'Stop, thief!' . . .

What causes us to redden with greatest shame under our

greying or vanished hair is the vileness of certain desires we had, the mere recollection of which sickens us.

Do not count too much on society to reform itself. Reform yourself.

And then, you ask, do we all become little saints?

No fear of that! I give you the rough outline of a vague programme, unrealizable. You will always be what you are, only a little less so. One can mitigate one's faults; one cannot get rid of them; but the small progress you make will illumine your life. You will walk with a lighter tread.

Someone who says, 'Thou, Reason, art my goddess,' is very likely to prove an imbecile.

Do not cling on to your every fault, on the pretext that perfection is not of this world.

17 March.

The inventor who patents a pleasure barometer – the needle indicates only fine weather, even when the weather is foul.

20 March.

Agricultural show. There is a stuffed owl. The budding young naturalist pulls a string: the owl turns its head, moves its eyes, spreads its wings. All of which the real owl did a good deal better while it was alive.

Rabbit skins, fanatically polished. Other rabbits in a queue, waiting their turn.

21 March.

I have a hydrocephalic head, and my ideas are constantly submerged under water. They reappear, but as if drowned.

22 March.

God will keep reminding us: 'You are not in Heaven to have fun.'

26 March.

Guitry, inside his immense and glacial automobile. He tells me that in the theatre I create *tours de force*, and I reply:
'Which cannot pierce the ears of the deaf.'
Then I announce, a little feverishly, my plan to write a three-act play about Philippe. He immediately offers me Le Breuil as a retreat, to work on it. I hold back from describing what I have in mind, for fear of not being clear.
'Basically,' I say, 'I have an overheated imagination. I have always kept it in check.'
'I know,' he said. 'The truth is your chosen medium, but imagination will have its day.'

I am becoming more modest, but also a little more haughty about my modesty.

4 April.

Artistes Indépendants. The place in the world where I am most bored. After pointillism comes building-block-ism, and a few young geniuses who take considerable pains to make the viewer throw up. It is as tedious as books of verse or prose published at the authors' expense. A salon to which no one is admitted, but anyone can enter.

In the midst of all of this, the head of a child by Paterne Berrichon, limpidly drawn and coloured, has the air, comparatively speaking, of a masterpiece.

7 April.

The obscure but impressive authority of a tailor who explains to you why an outfit, which suits you not at all, in fact suits you perfectly.

15 April.

Honorine: fingernails as long as you like. No longer hears, no longer recognizes anyone. We get her to eat. She is reverting to a plant, before she dies.

16 April.

Maman.

No, I will not lie about it. To the end, I will speak my indifference quite openly.

She arrives. Marinette invites her in and says: 'It's Grandmother.'

She kisses me (I cannot reciprocate), and sits down at once, without waiting to be asked. I say: 'Good morning, Maman, how are you?' Not another syllable. [. . .]

Outside, she kisses Marinette and thanks her. I am disconcerted. It is not that I am affected by her. Something else troubles me, not her. Of course! – it is she whom I will one day resemble. Grey hair that is still wavy, flesh that is going. Skin that covers the bones as best it can, and how pronounced they have become! And scab-like spots on her skin, like flaking paint on old wood.

Almost invariably, while it is happening, life bores or disgusts me. It is only afterwards that it arranges itself so as to amuse me.

19 April.

Honorine is huddled on top of her bed. She has not moved for two weeks. She says something which at first we do not catch. She shouts it out: 'Well go ahead and throttle me!'

A little embarrassed, all the same, at having married his wife's sister with such alacrity, he redoubles his pious attentions around her grave: it is the best-tended plot in the cemetery.

24 April.

The lark ascends, ascends. It will alight on the tip of God's finger.

10 May.

God did a fairly good job with nature, but He made a mess of man.

11 May.

I am no longer really alive. I seem like the reflection of a man in water.

15 May.

I have become lazy because Marinette was too afraid to point out to me that I do nothing.

Already my brain feels old, without elasticity.

17 May.

Do not write too concisely. One must help the public out with little flourishes of banality here and there. Daudet knew how to drop them in.

18 May.

I feel unreal, as if made of cloud, like one of those shapes which compose and decompose themselves at sunset.

I have the makings of a good priest, but am too anti-clerical ever to become a saint.

31 May.

Honorine lived so long that her death passed unnoticed. Sometimes, I think I still hear her step in the garden.

1 June.

We always end by despising those who agree with us too readily.

7 June.

Guitry passes through Chaumot.
What I always admire in him is his breeding, his subtle air of a gentleman.
But all of it enlisted in the service of the automobile, this unravelling of pleasure, this irksome liberty, which finds boredom at the bottom of everything . . . [. . .]
'Venice!' I say.
'So let's go!' he replies. I decline, but off he goes, without having given it a thought. [. . .]
He looks like an English gentleman, a greying Englishman, and prefers to be told that he looks like an American.

15 June.

Philippe scythes the hay, but cannot tell me the name of a flower. As the meadow is on a slope, he wears a clog on his left foot and a worn-out shoe on the right, so as not to slip. At the entrance to the meadow: waistcoat, hammer, anvil for straightening the scythe before sharpening it. And two different footprints in the grass.

16 June.

Patriotism. Sometimes the Nevers bull disdains to notice the existence of the dainty Breton cow.

17 June.

In the work of Flaubert, a subtle bouquet of boredom.

A socialist, yes, but I turn into a furious landowner when the children throw sticks into my cherry trees, and immediately talk of going to fetch my gun.

19 June.

Académie Goncourt. I only have time for political or religious discussion. Literary gossip bores me to death.

Contortions of a big caterpillar assailed by ants that clamber over it, eating its head, its belly, its eyes. Gulliver in Lilliput. Last desperate efforts: it stiffens and unbends itself like a bow. A final spasm: it is dead. The more timid ants now come running. It is black and swarming. They drag it under a strawberry plant.

All very well to be my age and a mayor: but when I see a policeman I still feel uneasy.

7 July.

Nietzsche. What do I think of him? I think that there are quite a few unnecessary letters in his name.

17 July.

Small town. Monsieur Judge and Monsieur Notary are having a good laugh because Monsieur Sub-Prefect went mushroom-hunting this morning, in this heat, and consequently has not found a single specimen.

30 July.

The tailor's dummy thinks she is the Venus de Milo because she has no arms.

6 August.

Philippe still does not know on which side the moon waxes and wanes, and on which side the horns point when it is in the first quarter. I tease him a little about his ignorance. His reply: 'I never look at the moon.'

Catholicism has habituated them to a sort of mechanical honesty with which they are contented. As long as you go to Mass you can tell lies. The Republic will fall prey to the same logic; they throw their statues of the Virgin into the stables, but continue to beat their wives.

The priest only wanted to dominate them. After which he was satisfied. He cared nothing for their moral education.

His lay equivalent will have many disappointments along the way.

To die is to extinguish the world.

'There were forty people at the baptism of Jules,' says Maman. There will not be as many at his funeral.
She also says: 'He was so pretty that everyone took him for a little girl.'

7 August.

As man, Christ is admirable. As God, on the other hand, one might ask: 'What! Is that all He was capable of?'

10 August.

I read over again some old letters I wrote to Marinette. One does not change. Migraines, work manias, doldrums, enthusiasms, and Marinette at the centre of it all.

11 August.

Marinette has given me everything. Can I say that I have given her everything? It seems to me that my egotism has remained fairly intact.

When I say to her, 'Tell me frankly . . .' she reads very well in my eyes just how far along that path she should go.

To her, I can openly refer to 'my works ... my good qualities ... my wit', and even, after the tiniest hesitation, 'my talent'. By now she finds this way of talking so natural that I use it without any constraint ...

I am not sure if she has improved me, apart from smartening me up.

At the thought that, on my account, she might fall into destitution, I feel a pang; and then, far too quickly, I tell myself: 'How well she would bear it! And she would love me even more.'

'I know what I have,' she says, 'and I would change places with no woman.'

16 August.

Our thought dashes itself against the great mystery, like a wasp against a windowpane. Less merciful than man, God never opens the window.

21 August.

Small town. The ironmonger's daughters prefer not to mix with the daughter of the confectioner. Iron is a nobler substance than confectionery – and besides, *they* would never be seen working in their father's store!

24 August.

After twenty years of service for Monsieur Perrin, Philippe received, from the agricultural association of Lormes, a medal and forty francs. He went on foot to collect them: thirty-five kilometres there and back. As for the forty francs, they have long since been spent, and he does not know what became of the medal.

Why on earth travel! There is nature, activity and history wherever you are.

31 August.

Although myself paraplegic, I am a severe judge of the gait of others.

3 September.

God, in His modesty, does not dare to boast of having created the world.

6 September.

My horror of lies has destroyed my imagination.

The profession of letters is, after all, the only one in which you can make no money without seeming ridiculous.

11 September.

Make a social novel out of them. But the peasant is not a hero in a novel. You may write a book about him, but not a novel. To speak of him you must renounce the old formulas. And don't count on making him utter as many idiocies as the bourgeois: he would not put up with it.

12 September.

To novelize the peasant is almost to insult his misery, his condition. The peasant has no story; or, at least, not a story in a novel.

These notes are my daily prayers.

15 September.

A schoolmistress refuses to take a husband who has 100,000 francs, because he looks like a labourer; and because, she says, she does not want a husband who is less educated than herself. In the letter in which she rehearses these airs, there are four spelling mistakes.

17 September.

An onion, blown-up and paunchy, like those clowns with thirty-six waistcoats.

22 September.

The miller's wife. She does everything. 'Petits! Petits!' to the chickens, 'Bibi! Bibi!' to the turkeys, 'Goulu! Goulu!' to the ducks, 'Tii! Tii! Tia! Tia!' to the pigs. She does everything. All the while keeping up a rapid-fire amiability, which seems to say: 'Make it quick! My poultry need me!'
You hear her clogs in the courtyard.
She makes the pig-feed herself, though it is man's work.

Next to her, the husband remains invisible. You might say that he spends his life being wafted asleep to the sounds of his mill turning.

No maid, but even so, she still does too much.

The farmer's wife, on the other hand, gives out orders. Neatness, cleanliness, and the affability of the mistress of an establishment. The stove shines so that you'd think it is never used. She makes excellent butter, much sought after. She is well dressed, almost invariably wearing some token of mourning. She has a daughter who is a proper young lady. Who has a critical eye. Who knows that their shed is too cramped and unsuited for milking the cows.

Jesus Christ had talent aplenty.

3 October.

I am convinced that, indolent as I am, I shall die at an advanced age while engaged in some febrile activity.

On the horizon, the moon, like a balloon, unencumbered, saying: 'Let go!' It lifts. The cables are cut.

Not a man, not a tree, not a branch could hang on to its net and secretly cadge a lift.

The logs beneath burn red, to keep it climbing.

It reaches a cloud, seems to get caught, stops moving.

It disappears behind a mass of banked clouds. Never to be seen again. Not that one, at least.

4 October.

Until now we have written of peasants solely for comic purposes. The time is over for laughter. We need to look closer, into the dregs of their miserable condition, in which there is no longer cause for mirth.

8 October.

The automobile lives off the animals of the road, chickens mostly. Every fifty kilometres it needs to eat at least one chicken.

17 October.

Bad luck is tiresome enough, but there is something abject about good luck.

20 October.

A sheep, its muzzle eaten away by who knows what canker, its teeth exposed – and yet a gentle and pitiful air withal, continually eating grass if only to clean its nose, all the while looking at you as if to ask: 'You who knows everything: is there nothing to be done for my poor nose?'

Honorine comes back to us! She revisits her home, during the night: the old people are certain of it. Her grandson puts on a brave face, and says, 'It's just rats,' but he quakes with fear.

3 November.

Let us give ourselves up to the universal law of total dispersal.

Let us not forget that the world makes no sense.

5 November.

What happens to all the tears that we do not shed?

16 November.

She is going to be married.
'I don't know why I said yes,' she says. 'I'd have been embarrassed to say no.'
It is not yet official. She says:
'I will marry when I'm no longer in mourning for Papa, so I can have a fiddler. And I want white slippers. You only have one day in this life to be beautiful.'

19 November.

Thadée Natanson tells me:
'There is a Monsieur who wants to set some of your *Histoires Naturelles* to music. He is an avant-garde composer, well regarded, for whom Debussy is already old hat. What do you think of the idea?'
'I think nothing.'
'Come, come! It must mean something to you.'
'On the contrary.'

'What shall I tell him?'
'Anything you like. Say thank you.'
'You don't want him to let you hear some of his music?'
'On no account!'

22 *November.*

I am in no great hurry to see the society of the future – our own is favourable enough for a writer. By its absurdities, its injustices, its vices, its stupidities, it nourishes a writer's observation. The more men improve, the more colourless man will become.

The little money I have allows me to scorn the rich and praise impoverished virtue. I use it to provide for myself and to say what I think. Would I be able to speak my mind if I did not have this small income, in other words this basic independence? Am I a racketeer? Do I enrich myself? Do I add more pennies to the pennies I have? No. I will spend everything on the cause that I defend. I may have had a well-off air: so much the worse for me if you were taken in; but I have spoken out against the rich and for the poor; I have been of service to poverty, and that is what matters.

The saddest moments: when you start to believe that all wisdom is a hoax.

29 November.

My books are so remote from me that I am already, so to speak, their posterity. So here is my verdict, plain and simple: I shall never read them again.

Marinette will be the dedicatee of my book. I tell her so. She replies, 'Marinette Immortalized,' with a smile of happiness. I think she cares not a fig for immortality, but cares a little for what I think of her.

2 December.

What about orgasm? Not coming is just as amusing, and less fatiguing.

The void is soundless. You have to be a great poet to make it echo.

4 December.

Antony. *Julius Caesar*. Perhaps for the first time I feel Shakespeare. Perhaps also because I always liked Brutus. The fate of an honest man who has failed! An evening like this is the recompense for our classical studies.

At each moment your spirit is capsized, your face a mask of tensed muscles. You can't help weeping. [...]

The speech of Mark Antony is amusing, but not very accurate. This was the age of Cicero. He would have distrusted all this melodrama. He'd have preferred the words of Brutus, of a perfect and noble simplicity. At two or three points he is wide of the mark to speak of his 'great heart', but his overbearing friendship for Cassius, his reaction to the death of his wife, what splendours!

Shakespeare's images are less literary than those of Victor Hugo, but more human. With Hugo, you sometimes see nothing but the image; with Shakespeare, you never cease to see the truth, the muscles and the blood of truth.

At times you would think you are listening to Racine. The French translation is in a rhymical prose. No rhymes: one is thankful for that, at least.

One should develop a taste for Shakespeare late in life, when one has tired of perfection.

5 December.

Yesterday evening, re-read *Julius Caesar*. I had read it but forgotten it. After the creation that is Antony, and after this reading, I understand why I used not to like Shakespeare. He is perhaps the playwright above all others who needs to be staged to be understood. It is enough to read Victor Hugo, but nothing of Hugo has taken possession of me on stage like *Julius Caesar*. Shakespeare is more a man of the theatre than Hugo.

You do not discover him: you discover yourself; you awaken in yourself an admiration for him that was always there but dormant.

1906

10 December.

Even in *Poil de Carotte* I did not dare to say everything. I did not include this: Monsieur Lepic sending Poil to ask Mme Lepic if she wants a divorce, and the reception he gets from Mme Lepic. What a scene that would have made!

14 December.

There is justice, but we do not always see it. Discreet, smiling, it is there, to the side, lagging a little behind injustice, which makes so much noise.

16 December.

With Guitry, who is making a lot of money, and signs cheques for 10,000 francs at a time. On very good form, telling stories about English comic actors.

The most amusing is the glass of water.

A man rushes on stage, shouting: 'A glass of water! Quick! Water!' Everyone jumps to attention: servants, waiters, maître d'hôtel ... Glasses are knocked over and smashed. Finally, he gets his glass of water – and sticks a carnation into it.

17 December.

I have reached an age where I can understand how deeply I must have offended my teachers (Alphonse Daudet) when I went to see them and never asked them about themselves.

19 December.

Sarah is no longer an actress. She is like the song of the trees, like the pitch of an instrument. It is perfect, and we are used to it.

22 December.

Penguins, the tips of their wings in the pockets of their waistcoats.

1907

4 January.

Marinette, seeing how quickly I pass from one mood to another, says: 'There are two of you.'

12 January.

Monsieur Ravel, the composer of *Histoires Naturelles*, dark, wealthy, distinguished, is insistent that I go this evening to listen to the song-cycle he has written.

I explain my ignorance and ask him to tell me what he found to add to the words of *Histoires Naturelles*.

'My intention was not to add,' he said, 'but to interpret.'

'But what connection is there . . . ?'

'To say with music what you would say with words, when you are in front of a tree, for example. I think in music and feel in music, and I should like to think and feel the same things that you do. There is instinctive, emotional music, such as mine – needless to say, the craft must first be learnt – and then there is intellectual music, such as that of d'Indy. This evening will be mostly of the d'Indy variety. They do not admit emotion because they do not want to analyse it. I believe the opposite; but they must be interested in what I am up to, because they admit me. This test is very important for me. One thing I am sure about is my singer: she is excellent.'

23 January.

What is a thinker? Unless he can give me an explanation of the universe, I care not a fig for his thinking.

12 February.

I understand life less and less, I love it more and more.

To the young. I am going to tell you an old truth which you may not like, because you prefer novelty. This truth is that one does not age. Where the heart is concerned, this is generally accepted, at least in matters of love. But it is the same with the mind. It remains forever young. You do not understand life any more at forty than you did at twenty, but you are aware of the fact, and you admit it. And to admit it is to remain young.

19 February.

Trip to Chaumot. Philippe's fingers tremble when he touches a sheet of paper. I should like to speak softly to him – but because he is getting deaf I must shout. I sound as though I were in a temper.

It is so cold that he no longer smells. His beard is frozen by the cold that comes down the chimney.

In the vegetable garden, only the indomitable leeks refuse to freeze. [...]

How would they manage to bring up their children if death did not help them out?

They have a certain savour when one visits them, in between catching trains. They are close to nature, as close to the soil as their animals. They live the silent life of leeks, and one marvels that they do not freeze.

28 February.

I like music, all kinds of music, the simplest and the most complicated, and the kind that so generously allows us to keep thinking of something else. It reminds me of the swaying of the poplars in my village, minus their leaves; and the canal where, at the behest of a wind without any ambition, the reeds bend and rise like the violin-bows of an orchestra, though with less noise.

The writer of prose is supposed not to need music. This is not the case: without it he would be nothing.

The conductor translates the music by means of a precise pantomime, like a great actor: receives a sudden blow to the solar plexus, plucks a note out of the air, says 'hush' with his finger to his lips, lunges forward, takes a dance step, bars the horizon with his baton extended, drops his arms: it is over.

Your heart, which you had supposed to be dry to the point of hearing it crackle, suddenly spills over with hot tears.

4 March.

How many actors seem natural, merely because they are entirely artless!

18 March.

The intrepid critic should take his seat wearing blinkers, like a submissive horse, or, if you will, a donkey.

22 March.

The theatre will be renewed only by those who understand nothing about it.

25 March.

Perhaps death takes us only when we are fully ripened: I take reassurance from my slow maturity.

How is one to believe that a servile soul can be immortal?

28 March.

God – another one who thinks himself immortal!

8 April.

Woman. Chewing discreetly, at the back of her mouth, like a horse with his head in his nosebag.

10 April.

Keep at arm's length those precepts which bring in a tidy profit.

1 May.

My fear, when I walk behind a woman: that she thinks I am following her.

I like the commonplace flower and the rare compliment.

2 June.

The art publisher, a gentleman who never pays his bills, as far as authors are concerned.

18 June.

The man of letters is someone who never has reason to complain, while knowing how to do without almost everything.

25 June.

We are put here in order to laugh.
In Purgatory or in Hell we shall no longer have reason to do so.
And in Paradise it would be improper.

They are true Christians, because they think their religion excuses everything.

26 June.

Death is the norm. We make too much of life.

10 July.

No one suffers on account of being less intelligent than his neighbour.

17 July.

It is harder to be honourable for a week than to be heroic for fifteen minutes.

19 July.

Maman calls her house 'le cottage'.

Migraine. This must be what Christ meant by His crown of thorns.

20 July.

Marinette at once angelic and demonic, in the midst of her preserving-pans.

A man who had an *absolutely clear* vision of the void would kill himself instantly.

23 July.

They write treatises on the habits of ants, but are astonished that I should observe my peasants from close up.

24 July.

He appears unannounced and hands me a letter. Written on the envelope: 'M. & Mme Renard, Mayor of Chitry.'

'Who sent you?' I do not wish to make a habit of not giving the poor a hard reception.

'Monsieur Perrin.'

I tear open the envelope. A letter, in which I read: 'Former gendarme ... lost his sight ...' and other things that I scan without comprehending, for I am thinking only of what I can possibly say to this man, and of the pages themselves, yellow and blackened, as if burnt by fire. Or by destitution.

'But you are Monsieur Perrin,' I say. 'And you say that he sent you?'

'Yes,' he says, smiling. 'I sent myself.'

He says it like a man who is alone in the world.

But he is on the road with a wife and three children. He lives in Mâcon. It is too late for him to continue to Corbigny: the *mairie* will be shut. They would not find anywhere to spend the night. He is asking for help.

'How do you live?'

'Since I lost my sight ...'

'But these small villages have no means to offer poor relief.'

'I know that.'

He has the air of a bandit but also of a poor bugger. I give him twenty sous.

'I can give him some bread,' says Marinette in a low voice.

He has heard. He waits.

'He has enough,' I say.

I say it harshly, like a bourgeois whose repose has been disturbed. And he has addressed me bare-headed, yet I have not bothered even to tip my hat. Why? Why?

30 July.

A thimble is the finest present you could give Marinette. Made of gold.

2 August.

They are afraid of my writing, that I might 'put' them in the newspapers; but as long as it is not the *Echo de Clamecy* they are not bothered.

3 August.

When I consider the appetites of the average bourgeois, I feel myself capable of doing without everything.

4 August.

The cat stands guard and dozes at the foot of the vine. Up above, there is a warbler's nest and three chicks who will fall out, sooner or later, if they do not calm down and sit still.

The cat waits.

This spider has spun its web beneath a flower. It catches nothing but petals. And is soon dead, thereby adding to its reputation for cruelty that of imbecility.

10 August.

Out walking. I see again the field where my godfather used to stoop among his vines. These oats are mine! These potatoes! 'Look at how rich you are!' says Marinette.
And here are two partridges, running across my property!
This is what one's native land amounts to: a minute of intense emotion, now and then, but not all of the time.

11 August.

I can see quite clearly my statue, on the old cemetery square, with this inscription:

JULES RENARD

from his indifferent countrymen

20 August.

The comet of August 1907. You can spot it quickly enough, in the east, from around two o'clock in the morning. It looks like a pale shooting star, arrested as it falls over the Narteau woods; also like a billiard cue flung into the sky.

With my lantern, my red dressing gown, my woollen shawl,

my visor on top of my cotton nightcap, I must look like an astrologer of old without his spectacles.

As luck would have it, the comet disappears behind a cloud. Nothing more monotonous than these marvels. [...]

On the horizon, shortly before sunrise, a star – Saturn or Jupiter. It is well worth a comet.

29 August.

The automobile: vertigo and boredom combined.

They immediately ask you what horsepower. Let's just say fifteen hundred and have done.

There are moments when, on a trip where all expenses are paid by the most generous of friends, one feels suddenly like a parcel.

Guitry salutes an ancient priest, who reciprocates, surprised and flattered.

'I must give him some money,' says Guitry, who runs up to him and says: 'Father, please accept this small offering. It is nothing, but may help alleviate the suffering of one of your poor.'

We laugh, and those watching do not know what to make of it, the performance is so immaculate. Anyone except Guitry would botch these little scenes. He is a man of letters who performs instead of writing. Even the slightest of his stories is played to perfection, as to gesture and pitch.

4 September.

Le Puy. They are a little ashamed of their gilded Virgin, and say that one gets used to her.

6 September.

The pig throws its ears ahead and follows them.

Never have I said to myself: 'I will make a note of this.' It is only afterwards that things come.

7 September.

Working women. Not all women are idle.

This one saved her husband the expense of a servant and handyman. She was always ill-tempered because her work was never done. In the end it killed her. [. . .]

This other one, exhausted, is sitting, almost lying, on the embankment. She is at the end of her tether, no strength left. She says:

'The peasant's lot is too hard. Why are there peasants?'

Her face is resigned, almost mean. Her husband, a stacker, earns good money. She might have been happy with him, but he drinks, and beats her. She sees nothing of what he earns. She has given up.

But then, on the back page of the newspaper, she sees an advertisement that will perhaps help her to get back her strength. She is going to take 'Pink' pills. It is her last hope. Who would take it from her?

12 September.

Ragotte, sixty-two years old, but still has a good appetite.

Her vanity lies in wanting to have us think that women eat

less than men. At noon, she eats less than Philippe, but she doesn't mention the fact that, at ten o'clock, she was standing in the courtyard with a slice of bread and cheese four centimetres thick. With her little knife she was cutting off 'quarters' that she could hardly swallow.

On Sundays she only makes a tiny lunch for Philippe, because he doesn't work on a Sunday.

16 September.

A fine sight, albeit imaginary: the honest lawyer who asks for a conviction for his client.

18 September.

What visitors to our region most admire is not me: it is the whiteness of our oxen.

20 September.

In the middle of the night: a horse suddenly laughed out loud.

26 September.

In the path, the caterpillar playing a soundless little tune on its accordion.

1907

6 October.

Politics ought to be the finest thing in the world: a citizen at the service of his country. Instead of which it is the meanest thing.

10 October.

I ask Baïe to fetch my notebook and pencil: 'I'm on my way,' shouts Baïe. 'Hang on to your idea, Papa!'

Every day I am by turns child, man and old crone.

28 October.

If we were able to – not so much fix, but prolong – the moments of emotion experienced through music, we should be more than mere men.

I promise Fantec fifty francs if he passes his examination.
'What will you buy with it?'
'A skull.'

4 December.

Prix Goncourt. I have never been given a prize. I would have liked to be offered one.

Mariette no longer feels like washing dishes or polishing shoes. She would like to be a shop assistant. It is an idea that worries away at her, that grows of its own accord. She hopes that Marinette will help her.

She does not know how to do multiplication.

'But in life you get to where you want to get,' she says.

This is all that she learnt in school.

She has no complaint about her life here. She knows that she would not earn more elsewhere, but there is no regret, no trace of affection for us, who have treated her like a daughter of the house.

1908

3 January.

A window onto the street is worth an entire theatre.

7 January.

I should like to see something sadder than myself; the animals in the zoo, for instance.

8 January.

If my books bore painters as much as their paintings bore me, I can forgive them.

When I am in front of a picture, it speaks better than I do.

9 January.

It is even harder for me to settle my moods than my accounts.

Writing for someone is like writing to someone: you immediately feel obliged to lie.

There is also a sort of calculated originality, which one sees coming, which feels commonplace, which leaves us cold.

You must live to write, not write to live.

10 January.

Voltaire was an admirable businessman, which explains why he did not remain the poet he believed himself to be.

Shadow lives only in light.

A cloud sails along as though it knew where it was going.

11 January.

Mme Danville, a charming woman, flirts with abstract ideas, smokes, exhales through her nose. A husband could be unfaithful with impunity. His wife would say: 'Goodness, dear, how you reek of tobacco!' – safe in the assumption that he had spent his evening with friends.

13 January.

My strokes of good fortune, nearly always by mistake.

The danger of success is that it makes us forget the vile injustice of the world.

When we were both eighteen, he was youth and wealth and

happiness personified. I just ran into him in the street. We recognized one another and looked away. He is no longer young. His features have lost their delicacy. His clothes have lost their elegance. What he must see in the mirror is not the moustache but the pimples.

Making his way unhurriedly to his office in the Crédit Lyonnais.

He seemed destined to do nothing. What went wrong? What became of his father? Or his mother, who put on such airs and came of the nobility but ran a café herself, without needing to? Because you have to keep yourself busy in this life!

One's taste ripens at the expense of one's happiness.

It should not be thought that idleness is unproductive. Inside it you live intensely, like a hare listening.

You swim in its element, as in water; and are brushed lightly by the grasses of self-reproach.

16 January.

Ah, Marinette, no ill-humour! You should always be cloudless. On your clear brow the least shadow would be a stain.

'But I am tired; and besides, I am irritable.'

If you are tired, take a rest. Tiredness suits you, but not irritability.

The least ill-humour on your part is unbearable for me. If for one instant you give me your little wooden stare, all is ruined. I can only bear to see you in good spirits, gentle, kempt, and in the pink of health. Try never to stop being all of these things.

Thus, by dint of sheer egotism, do I succeed in turning you into an ideal wife.

19 January.

Oh, for something new! A new sensation, even if it consist of my own death.

The naturalists, like Maupassant, observed just a little of life and filled in the rest, imagination and art serving to complete the thing observed.

As for us, we no longer dare to rearrange anything. We count on life to bring life to completion. And if life is in no hurry, we wait.

For them, life was not sufficiently literary. For us, it is literary enough as it is.

23 January.

Third Goncourt dinner. [. . .] Rosny gets to his feet, and for a quarter of an hour talks of scientific progress, of what makes us superior to our fathers, of substance and inertia, of true matter being the void, and of what we used to call matter as merely an interruption of the void. He quotes Bergson. He sounds like a man of integrity, a man of force. His intellect impresses us.

'In short,' he says, 'our abstract ideas about the universe are now more worked out than those of our fathers.'

'We have simply found other connections between sensations,' says Poincaré, 'but what is sensation if nothing exists?'

'Some things we have forgotten,' adds Daudet. 'We do not

know what the Greeks thought. We have lost it all. They perhaps employed better instruments than ours. The world consists of forgetting.'

'And Rosny,' I say, 'has spoken to us for a quarter of an hour without mentioning the word "ethical". But therein lies our question, our point of departure.'

'Man is no better than he was.'

'Shall we try and see,' says Poincaré, 'if he is any better in the matter of going to sleep?'

And we go our separate ways.

Scruples, the parasites of the will.

28 January.

Ah, no! I am not one of those who has to go to Venice to experience an emotion.

Under attack from all sides, God defends himself by resorting to contempt: by not answering the charges.

I give the impression of a fulfilled life, but I have done almost nothing of what I set out to do.

30 January.

It is always better to keep quiet. One says nothing by speaking. Either the words outrun the thought or they diminish it. In the former case, what nerve! In the latter, what timidity and excess of scruple!

31 January.

Someone who believes in nothing can also be the very pattern of an honourable man.

3 February.

Every morning, on waking, you should say: 'I see, I hear, I move, I am not in pain. Thank you! Life is beautiful.'

It is what our character makes of it. We fashion it, as a snail its shell.

7 February.

I could publish a volume of all the letters I have written and not posted.

9 February.

Belief in work is perhaps yet another useless religion. One is happy only by chance.

11 February.

Salle Wagram. Boxing. Not very interesting. Some crude parrying, close in, and sly rabbit punches to the left side of the body, to make breathing difficult.

Small mysterious noises made by Tristan, the expert, as he watches.

What is moving is to see a man on the ground, not getting up, but waiting for the referee to finish the count.

What is amusing is to see how, when the referee cries 'Stop!' at the end of a round, each boxer goes to his corner, sits on his stool and has himself fanned with towels like an Indian prince.

Wiped down, massaged, sponged.

They are ugly, their features flattened. Tristan admires the powerful sloping shoulders: he also presumably admires the vast neck planted in the shoulders. He shakes hands with various shaven-headed individuals who smell of the stables. Darzens has a black patch over his left eye. It seems he put out his eye while turning a bicycle wheel and inspecting the pedal too closely. Ah, these sportsmen!

At the Medical Faculty, the attendant says: 'Well, if you want me to be good to you, you'll have to cross my palm.'

Then he adds:

'And what I just said is not to be repeated.'

Fantec gives him forty sous. Otherwise, the attendant assigns you a cadaver that is too fat to dissect; you also have to pay him for the cadaver: a hundred sous, I think.

And you have to pay for a locker, and pay for your smocks to be bleached, twice as expensive as at home.

12 February.

During the war, a man resigns himself to eating his dog, Médor, then looks at the leftovers and says: 'Poor Médor! How he'd have feasted on the bones!'

18 February.

Trip to Chaumot, from the 14th to the 17th.
They have no idea how long a cow can live. As soon as they think she might be old, they fatten her up and sell her to the butcher.

21 February.

Tomorrow I shall be forty-four. Which is no sort of age. It's only at forty-five that you need to start thinking; at forty-four you are still walking on air.

Note: there is no entry, for last year, on being forty-three; clearly forty-three held no worries.

22 February.

Forty-four is when you begin to give up hope of doubling before quitting.

I feel old, but would not wish to be younger by as much as five minutes.

25 February.

My ignorance and my admission of ignorance, these are the better part of my originality.

1908

12 March.

The theatre. We applauded. What clappings! Our box was as noisy as a wash-house.

27 March.

Maman is obsessed by taking care of herself and living another fifty years.

To read again the poetry you once knew by heart.

4 April.

Zola immoral? But he stinks of morality! Coupeau gets punished, Nana is punished, all the villains in Zola get their comeuppance.

16 April.

The flight of a pigeon landing on a branch that is too frail. With its wings it buoys up the branch.

2 May.

Ostrich: a giant chick.

14 May.

I always want reason on my side – but one reason is never enough, even if it is the best: I need a straight flush of reasons.

In politics, sincerity has the air of a complicated and suspicious manoeuvre, a clever bit of duplicity.

16 May.

What spoils the Bois de Boulogne is the rich. And the horseback riders who enjoy making their saddles squeak! And the poor old men doing a spot of cycling before they die!
Governesses sitting on benches and reading books that are always in tiny print. Ruining their eyes.
The Bois, which at the moment makes me weep with joy, leaves me, not with a wish to return, but with a longing for the country.
How few people there are who can look at something beautiful without the automatic thought that they can now say: 'I saw something beautiful!'

25 May.

When a man has proved that he has talent, he still needs to prove that he knows how to use it.

26 May.

My name printed in a newspaper lures me like a scent.

1908

31 May.

Descaves shows me one of his son's dictation exercises. From Jules Renard's *La Louée*. Descaves junior says: 'Oh, a passage of Jules Renard, that's easy-peasy: no one ever makes mistakes.'

The Abbey of Valloires, which you can never find on a map. A pretty ruin. Panelling, a chapel with a screen worth a lot of money. On the ceiling, a morel fungus reminds us that there was one growing on the spot when the chapel was built. Everything reverts to nature. Gardens in flower, trees of great beauty. These monks knew how to live: be useless.

9 June.

She thought herself the beautiful blonde of Chitry. She goes to Paris, sees the handsome whores, appraises herself in the shop mirrors and decides that she falls short of perfection. Returning to Chitry, she admits it openly.

'I am less beautiful in Paris than I am here,' she says, 'but I think it has something to do with the mirrors.' [...]

The pride of the slut who reappears in her village, and makes her entrance at the ball. All the girls, under the expert eye of the mayor, cast envious sidelong glances at her.

'Which goes to show that virtue is not rewarded,' says Baïe.

'In her métier, my girl, you do not have to be virtuous', say I.

I do not want to sort peasants into different categories. They are all the same. Their brain has an air of working more slowly than ours, which is merely to say: in a different manner. They have their pride, a particular form of stupidity. I take note of this. But, to my mind, their poor impoverished language is what is least original.

It is the patois of their thought that amuses me, not of their speech; it is their soul, not their outward particulars.

17 June.

Men are always on the run from God, who does not know how to tame them.

Fame is the smoke without fire that we hear so much about.

18 June.

Sheep cough like old men.

21 June.

It is perhaps in the privy that, out of tedium, I have written my best thoughts.

26 June.

In this obscure corner of the world we call a village, all of humanity, more or less, is to be found.

The idea of you being dead makes me immediately want to die. One day, still very much alive, you will find me dead.

If I were to be unfaithful to you with another woman, I would be looking your way all the while.

I have loved you as a natural force, I have looked at you as at a magnificent tree, I have inhaled you as a hedge in bloom, I have savoured you like a plum or a cherry.

You are happiest when there rains on your beautiful face a storm of kisses.

They bring him a pair of shoes to mend.

'Very good, Madame,' he says. 'I will hand these over right away to one of my assistants.'

Poor man, there is no one else.

5 July.

The true egoist would even allow others to be happy, on condition that he is the cause of their happiness.

7 July.

Vanity is the spice of life.

28 July.

'My house intern,' says Fantec, 'has become aware that I am your son. He went to the Comédie-Française. He saw *Le Plaisir de Rompre*. He said: "Are you vaguely related in some way to this Jules Renard?" I replied: "Vaguely, yes."'

'He must have vaguely thought you were boasting.'

30 July.

First sighting of Augustine, who is about to become part of our life. A solid farm girl in appearance. She came 'on foot'. I wonder that she didn't bring her cow. She was employed by the café owners in Corbigny. They refused to give her a reference. The wife, who has her troubles, is fond of white wine.

She says, as they all do: 'You can say whatever you like to me.'
Augustine adds:
'But if you swear at me, I'll cry.'

Her big, not-too-bright girlish face lights up at the prospect of seeing Paris. She smiles.

'I'd like to see what all the fuss is about. But not to stay there for long; I'd come straight back to the country.'
'Do you know anyone there?'
'I have a cousin who works in the rue de Sèvres.'
'It's not very near to where we will be.'
'Oh, that doesn't matter.' [. . .]

Just enough education to make a good illiterate of her, in three or four years, when she will have forgotten what she has learnt, which was next to nothing.

A pockmarked face, well scrubbed with laundry soap.

She will come to us with her little bundle, into a house where there are four strangers, without counting Philippe and Ragotte, who may turn out to be enemies – yet it is we who take precautions against her! It is we who are afraid and mistrustful!

'I like her better than the other one,' says Ragotte. 'The other one wore too many flounces.'

Books have lost their savour for me. They no longer teach me anything. It is as though one were to suggest to a painter that he copy a painting. Nature! you are all that is left.

4 August.

The perfect book. I could write it, if I would.

When she was twelve, Augustine was earning forty francs a year, on a farm. The kind of situation, she says, from which a girl leaves 'in trouble', that is, pregnant.

Attracted and troubled by Paris. She is afraid of being murdered there.

'Is there an attic in which to dry the washing? You can't dry it outside in winter.'

'Neither attic nor outside: the laundress brings it back all dry, ironed and folded.'

'Then what will we do, the maids, in Paris?'

She has four chemises. She will buy six more with her next wages. She asks if, in Paris, we have a cow.

She does not read newspapers: she is too afraid.

'Ever since I came here,' she says, 'every day I eat something new. If I'd been running since the last time I had roast chicken to eat, I'd be a long way off by now!'

12 August.

A bat always seems to be flying between four walls.

26 *August.*

I have never been able to stop myself from rescuing a fly caught in a spider's web.

Augustine, having risen late, arranged everything to her satisfaction by setting the clock back three-quarters of an hour.

28 *August.*

I am by nature neither an observer nor a wit. I see little, and my replies are true, which is to say, slow in coming. It is only afterwards that everything falls into place.

Philippe always looks upon the dog as a dog. I, on the other hand, am perhaps too inclined to take it for a man.

Not only am I not observant, but I am afraid of observing, and I deliberately let go many admirable and noteworthy things regarding my family. I refuse to look, I prefer to turn aside.

I have the wit of a ruminant. Chewing the cud of recollection is what amuses me.

21 *September.*

Pure theatre, which is to say pure falsehood.

Art is an education: it gives the reader eyes.

Reverie is my fertilizer.

Art: nudges truth along a little, with its finger.

22 September.

A critic is rather like a soldier who fires on his own regiment, or who crosses over to the side of the enemy, the public.

25 September.

You must give yourself with an open mind to every experience. You must admire a religious ceremony if it is beautiful, rather than like it or hate it because it is religious.

We received our first ideas, and formed our taste, on books whose opening page had been torn out, leaving us ignorant of both author and title. It is the old dog-eared novel, read forty times in secret, that has had the most lasting influence on us.

26 September.

To portray man. What does that mean? One ought to paint the depths, but we cannot see them. We observe the exterior only. Now, there is no man, even the greatest, whose exterior – words and attitudes and gestures – do not show him to be fairly ridiculous. We retain only what is ridiculous. Art is pitiless, has no respect for virtue, and the conclusion of art, in all its forms, is that life seems above all to be a comedy.

Our admirations, about which we are so far from confident... Merely a 'Really, so you actually liked it?', aimed by almost anyone, is enough to throw us off kilter. Perhaps we were wrong, after all. From there to throwing admiration overboard is a short step.

29 September.

I travel incognito, needlessly so.

1–10 October.

Trip to Bayonne. Landscape nearly blackened by the sun. Heavy dust on the leaves: the hedges are white with it, and it is not hawthorn.

I like Les Landes, between Bordeaux and Dax. Russet ferns and red heather, clearings between the pines. It is both sad and inspiriting.

Bare trees, with a dried bouquet at their foot, planted in the villages. Sée cannot tell me their name.

Bullfight: sad, sinister and disgusting sight. Sée skirts the issue by saying this is a poor example of a bullfight. That much is clear!

The matador takes off his hat and throws it into the air behind him, before striking the bull in the correct spot. For the public, a dangerous moment. With a shake of its shoulder the bull throws off the sword, a poor thrust, and it lies where it falls.

Rostand was in attendance for the final fight. He hid himself at the back of his box, for fear of not being recognized. I did not visit him in Cambo. He would perhaps have read aloud his *Chantecler*. To be the only person who has read this piece, what a responsibility!

Game of pelota: violent, monotonous and sad.

1908

12 October.

'You are a great favourite,' says Mellot. 'A lot of people like you, and you are unaware of it – they are embarrassed to tell you.'

'Yes, I know. What they like me for, in the first place, is my gift, and the compliment cannot always be reciprocated.'

Sée has never looked at the moon. On the seashore I improvise an extempore course in astronomy, in my vague fashion.

'I am grateful,' says he. 'When I see Picard I will tell him, "The moon is a dead star!"'

15 October.

In the realm of friendship, hypocrisy can survive indefinitely. In matters of love, words are not enough: one must act. Friendship can survive for a long time without proofs.

In Nevers there is a street called rue du Renard. It's a start. After I die, people may mistakenly think it is named after me.

18 October.

Chantilly. Fine swans, their backs too round, the rudder of the tail a little heavy and thick, but graceful and white all the same, pure white except for the red beak and the feet gloved in black, like the arms of Yvette Guilbert. [...]

Ducks in take-off, rapid and steep, bearing telegrams for the reeds.

20 October.

Capus comes up with a formula for success: 'Personal worth multiplied by circumstance.' He is getting there.

23 October.

When the defects of others are perceived with so much clarity, it is because one has them oneself.

30 October.

From time to time I remember once having been a man of letters.

31 October.

There are moments when everything turns out right. Don't worry: they pass.

2 November.

A remark must say more than a page: otherwise it is useless.

24 November.

Ah! what fine things I would write in a journal intended for no reader!

27 November.

What surprises me most is that my heart keeps on beating.

22 December.

In our friendships, as in our loves, there is somewhere a raging bull on the loose.

24 December.

Peasants. In winter, they sleep and breathe, curled up like snails.

God. 'He feedeth the birds of the air.' And then in winter He lets them starve to death.

My attitude towards peasants has been the same as towards nature, towards animals, water, trees.
What I say about one tree applies to all trees, but it is only by looking at this tree, and not any other, that I find the image that will convey an impression to the reader.

28 December.

The old maid devoted to her dog.
'Mademoiselle, your dog stinks,' says a gentleman.
'No, Monsieur: it is I.'

1909

16 January.

Marinette, her luminous expression when she lights a rum omelette.

23 January.

Endowed with a fortunate memory, which allows me instantly to forget whatever I read.

I have reached the point of distrusting my distrust.

1 February.

Mots d'écrit. I have just re-read it. What comes naturally is love of truth. The odious imagination corrupts everything it touches.

9 February.

Mendès died yesterday, run over by a train. He was a witty man, and he detested irony.
Why should his death sadden me? I was always indifferent to him.

He reproached Rostand for his negligence.

'You can tell him so,' he suggested to me, 'you know him well.'

A producer, perhaps; a craftsman, no.

A vanity so prodigious that it could not have been contained in verse.

Next to him one felt mediocre; a few steps away from him and you felt perfectly reconciled to being mediocre.

A man for whom the outside world did not exist.

His conversation was like his duelling; he beat the air with his sentences, he left himself exposed. You could not bring yourself to puncture him with a rejoinder.

He was a poet, with something of the bourgeois. Like a bourgeois who has succeeded, he despised those of more limited means.

He believed in the common man, on whom he had never bestowed so much as a glance.

They said he was as handsome as a god. No one ever tried to say he was as handsome as a man.

Mendès. Streets full of people at his funeral. All looking out for themselves. Already asking each other: 'Have you prepared something?' Richepin speaks up for the poetry. Capus asks me have I something in mind for when it's my turn.

We clamber over the tombstones. A warden shouts at us to step down.

'You must understand, my good man ...' someone starts telling him.

'What I understand, is that you should not be clambering over tombs. And there are those here who ought to understand this better than I do.'

The son of Verlaine is pointed out, a big strapping youth, who is in charge of one of the Paris metro stations.

Mendès was everything I dislike, perhaps everything I envy.

16 February.

A new maid. Marie. Puts her faith in the number thirteen and does not work on Sundays. At thirty-eight, she is no more advanced than she was at thirteen. She was married once, and feels that once is enough.

She remembers only one good position, at the Spanish embassy. She has been in homes where the coffee was carefully measured out, and where her dinner consisted of a hard-boiled egg when the masters, who were wealthy, dined out.

She eats the crusts of the day before. She hasn't tasted fresh bread for a year. Shy, with an Alsatian accent and a lisp, she begs pardon each time she passes in front of your armchair.

25 February.

Jean Rostand, wonderfully intelligent, though not gifted like his brother Maurice, who composes sublime verses. Very moved, he recites for us some beautiful lines on the death of a friend, then goes off and plays with the young girls – Baïe, Juliette and poor little Michel. They are his audience:

'I am ugly, but I have magnificent teeth, and am highly intelligent. Do you like to flirt? Do you have a tennis court at Chitry? Would you like to waltz? I have a break six times a day, six cups of tea. You do not play golf? So what do you do instead? Besides, you are all three of you pretty, would you like me to find you husbands? Dark or blond, which do you prefer? Tell me, does Ragotte dye her hair? Is Lucienne beautiful? Is her husband handsome?'

28 February.

Literature is a calling in which you have to keep proving your talent to people who have none.

Good taste can also mean fear of life and fear of beauty.

4 March.

Goncourt dinner. Rosny, who considers Hugo a cretin of genius, a monumental imbecile, endeavours to explain to me what a thinker is, and the value of free thought: Kant, Bergson, Poincaré. And I persist in telling him that, in a line of poetry by Hugo, at his best, there is more thought than in any work of metaphysics.

10 March.

There is false modesty; there is no false pride.

25 March.

So now they are analysing little bottles of my urine, and it seems I have albumin in my blood. And, by means of a gadget that is a cross between a compass and a watch, Renault takes my blood pressure, and the needle shows twenty. It is too high. My heart, although the arteries are supple, beats too fast. I shall have to start taking notes on my old age.

7 April.

Peasants. They never eat eggs. Except as children, when they are still going to school; but they go off them as soon as they are grown-up. Besides, eggs can be sold, they bring in money.

Ragotte's stew. In an earthenware casserole, melt two or three lumps of bacon fat and then remove from the heat (important not to leave for too long: the bacon, being old – especially if you kill only one pig a year – will have a rancid taste); then mince together onion, garlic, shallots, carrots, potatoes, over which you pour a pot of water, throw in a fist of salt, cover with a lid, and it will be ready by noon.

The carrots do not cook as quickly as the potatoes; they are still hard when the stew is served.

My thoughts are scattered, like a flock of geese.

It is the brain that is ageing.

To tire myself out, I had no need to go down the path of excess. Can this sort of life be prolonged for much longer?

I might have written a half-dozen more books, not one of which any better. It seems to me that I have spent my life asleep.

My pen is already becoming too indolent to write. Is my brain having trouble in forming a thought?

19 April.

To write without thought for the future – 'from one day to the next'. This does not mean every day.

20 April.

Perfect weather. And to think that on such a day people are still dying!

My faithfulness as a husband, a comical thing, which adds to my literary reputation.

26, 27 April.

The lighthouse at Gatteville. They spend the whole year up to their necks in water, but they never eat fish. They live off the fowl who wheel around the lighthouse and shatter themselves against the lantern.

You have no right to take water from the sea – which is theft from the State, on account of the salt.

4 May.

Goncourt dinner. The idea of proposing us all en bloc for the Nobel Prize, each represented by his best work. The French Academy to propose the candidates: why should we not propose them ourselves?

One must write as one breathes. A long flowing breath, with its natural rhythms, by turns slow and hurried – that is the index of a good style.

All that is owed to the reader is clarity. He must accept originality, irony, violence, on our terms, even if he does not like it, or them. He has no right to judge of these matters. You might say they are not his concern.

Swinburne. Have tried reading some of his verses. Of a vapidity! Neither arresting nor original. Insipid. I am bored.

5 May.

I give thought to others only during my hours of indolence; on the other hand, I am naturally indolent.

Luxembourg Gardens: nothing but a dome of leaves under which people dream.

The way the whores smile at one. It is charming. It is born and dies with such rapidity! Brief flashes of warmth.

11 May.

Galerie Durand-Ruel. *Les Nymphéas*: a series of waterscapes, by Claude Monet. Nothing occurs to me. Obviously, they are pretty; but I cannot very well say: 'Very pretty, especially the oval frames.' There is an abyss between this art and mine.

A young man, shabbily dressed, sits gazing fixedly through half-closed eyes. I would dearly like to see what he sees.

It is painting for women – who cannot argue with it. It is too pretty: nature is not pretty.

A terrible urge to walk out, as if returning from a voyage, to be able to say: 'I was there.'

I can no longer walk from one end of the Tuileries to the other. I am obliged to sit down and give two sous to the old women who sell lilies-of-the-valley.

Philippe writes that Maman is no longer always in her right mind.

15–19 May, Chaumot.

Maman. Her illness, the armchair her stage. She gets into bed when she hears Marinette's footsteps.

Her moments of lucidity. When her acting is at its finest. She trembles, she rubs her hands together, her teeth chatter, and, with eyes slightly wild, she says: 'All there is to do! I'll get down to it right away. I'll set to work. When you work . . .' And she puts a darn in a stocking.

A handsome old woman, still: the face of a witch with sharp features, or of an old woman in a gypsy caravan, with her wavy white hair.

If we send her asparagus she gives it to the rabbits.

The women flock to her like thieves. She has not a chemise left, or a sheet: she has given everything away.

Finally, she says: 'I don't need money any more.' [. . .]

Three states: lucidity, enfeeblement, and actual suffering. In her lucid state, she is still entirely Mme Lepic.

She sends Philippe to tell us:

'Don't leave! I feel that I am fading!'

In her way of holding your hands and pressing her nails into them, there is almost an intent to wound.

22 May.

Happiness is the search for happiness.

'When winter comes,' he says, 'I feel like getting married. It is cold, the restaurant is a long way off, and I feel the need of a home. But when spring comes, it passes.'

24 May.

A walk to Chatou.

In the grass, a small woman, air of self-sufficiency. She has come a long way on a bicycle, with a black poodle. She is making a bouquet of yellow flowers. The poodle guards her. When she has finished, she moves on. Happiness, found in activity and unconcern. [...]

Yesterday I witnessed true happiness: after a day of burning heat, a cluster of rose bushes were receiving a continuous spray from a sprinkler. 'Oh yes! More! Oh, that feels good!' they were saying with all their leaves.

On a little square which overlooks the Seine they used to hang people. There are still the holes in which the gallows were planted. You could see the hanged man from a great distance.

It is fine writing, 'beautiful' descriptions, that gave me a taste for terseness, for three words in a row.

I have the conviction that a celibate humanity would be infinitely superior.

31 May.

Generous individuals keep their spare change jingling loosely in their waistcoat pockets; as easy to lose it as to spend it. As for me, I draw coins singly from the bottom of my prudently fastened purse.

2 June.

What might be termed the suspicious nature of Dame Justice, always on the alert.

5 June.

If celibacy is not a virtue, it is certainly a force.

11–16 June, at Chaumot.

Maman wants to go and see the leaves floating in the well, to sit on the kerb-stone. In her cupboard, she keeps something that she consults from time to time. Wild-eyed, she gets up suddenly from her armchair and goes into the garden.

Her legs, swollen with varicose veins, painful to look at. Her head is still handsome, with wavy hair, with only a hint of white here and there.

29 June.

Heredity. Trying to piece together the grandfather and grandmother from hearsay. This one says: 'She was malign.' – Another says: 'Oh, I knew him well!' – A third says: 'Oh! my memory is gone.' Impossible to make a chain of solid links: you must add imaginary links.

15 July.

Chaumot. Today, too much playing at emotions.

'Forgive me! Forgive me!' says Maman to me. She holds out her arms and draws me to her. She falls at the feet of Marinette, whom she has always ignored. She throws herself at the feet of Amélie, of her two daughters.

To these appeals for 'forgiveness', all I can find to say is: 'I'll come back tomorrow.'

Afterwards, she gives herself violent cuffs to the head with her fist.

August.

On the 5th, death of Maman, buried on the 7th. Visit from Capus. He had an automobile accident at Lormes. He arrives all fired up by his accident, in the midst of ours. 'Here, of course,' he tells me, 'you are under the influence of the central plateau.'

Last recorded words of my mother:
'Will you come back and see me soon? Thank you for coming.'

Mme Robin and Juliette had just gone. Baïe, Marinette and I left her alone, seated on the garden bench. Amélie had followed us in. I had just received the telegram from Capus announcing his visit. From her bench, she kept turning around in my direction, trying to guess what the telegram might be about.

I do not believe that she threw herself down the well. She had gone to sit on the kerb, having exchanged a few words with a passer-by. She tied the chain; then, the seizure. She toppled backwards. A little fellow on a cart, passing close by, saw it all. Amélie's maid heard a *plop!* She saw her down the well, she said, fallen on her back, and she screamed.

I come running on leaden legs. I pass others who are running. I throw off my hat and my Rostand cane. I bend over the edge of the well.

Skirts floating on the surface, a slight eddying such as there is when one has drowned an animal. No human face.

Of course I want to go down in the bucket at the end of the chain. The chain is rolled up. My boots are absurdly long and they turn up at the toes, the way fish do at the bottom of a pail.

Cries of 'Don't go down!' And another voice saying: 'It is not dangerous!'

At last, a ladder is brought. I can hardly get my feet free of the bucket. The ladder does not reach to the bottom. With one hand, I try to seize this dead thing that does not move. The head is under water. The dress tears. I come up again. All I did was wet my feet. What must I have looked like, coming up from the well?

Two men go down. They manage to catch hold of her and bring her up.

A fearful sight, her face, emerging from the well.

She is carried to her bed. Marinette is still here.

Not a tear. I behave mechanically, as if I were carefully controlling myself.

Spent the night with the body, as I did for Papa. Why? The same thoughts.

Whether she committed suicide or died by accident, what difference from a religious standpoint? In the one case, it is she who did wrong, in the other case, it is God.

A consecrated grave awaits her. Who will win the toss, the bigot or the freemasons?

One of her slippers still hasn't been found.

What is left? Work.

The slightest vexation overwhelms me, whereas a material event, such as an accident, a death, does not affect me. I would prefer to be affected.

'A tragedy, a dreadful tragedy.' Why, no! It does not take shape immediately like physical pain. There is pain after the event, which takes its own time to penetrate, to settle in.

The thunder at the edge of a dense cloud claims my attention.

We are not even responsible for our sorrows.

Is the fact that God is incomprehensible really the strongest argument for His existence?

Embarrassment in the face of sorrow is what marks us out most strongly as men of letters. The slightest thing is enough to bring it on: a telegram of condolence from a stranger.

She was being girlish, bending over the edge in order to see the wet ferns glistening down there, kneeling in order to alarm Amélie, exclaiming and raising her arms in the air so the maid would come running; then saying she was only chasing a hen out of the garden. The mother of an ironist should never make jokes.

No, it was not play-acting, although I was the first to think that this was exactly what it looked like . . .

Death is no artist.
Unfathomable accident.
The slow play of moonlight on the bedsheet.
Not a scratch on her. She must have dropped like a stone.

I recall Barrès telling me that other people in mourning always made him laugh.

22 *August*.

The black untruth of mourning.

As long as the world continues to be ridiculous!

Truth always disenchants. Art is there to give the lie to it.

An old woman knitting in the ditch behind her cows. She gets up.
'Monsieur Jules,' she says, 'I can show you a fine covey of partridges.'
'Where would that be?'
'Over there, in the stubble. They ran ahead of me, big juicy ones.'
'But I have given up hunting, my good woman.'
'You no longer hunt?'
'No. I leave that to the young.'
'Oh, you are not so old!'
'But I am getting there, dear lady. To every dog his day.'
'What a shame. Big fat ones! I've never seen such beauties.'
(What to do? Give her money? Thanking her does not seem enough.)
'I no longer hunt,' I say, 'but next year I'll hunt.'

'But next year you will be even older.'

We are getting into a proper muddle here. She sits down again, disappointed.

'Thank you kindly, all the same.'

'Oh! it's nothing.'

Life is neither long nor short: it has its *longueurs*.

22 *October*.

One must spare one's heart so as to fortify one's judgement.

23 *November*.

Goncourt dinner.

We discuss the vileness of the world. Perhaps the only virtue of the Académie Goncourt: candour.

Daudet describes a salon, during which a length of string appeared from under the skirts of one of the women present. They pulled on it: it was a tapeworm. Bourges appalled by the story.

Crisis. Shortness of breath; disgust with everything. Death may come in an hour or in a decade. And to think that I should prefer the latter!

Once again, my balance is destroyed. I touch the bottom. Instant recovery, if only I could work.

As death approaches, we smell of fish.

27 November.

Romanticism is when you make the animals speak and they say what you want them to say. Realism is when you submit to their nature, which is not to speak.

How can anyone be allowed to set up as a critic, without even passing a spelling test?

From today, all my thoughts are tinged with death.

The effort one makes to resist giving in to a powerful emotion, because we know it to be false.

The heartless man, who has only ever known literary emotions.

5 December.

Saw Rostand again, after nine years. I kiss him on the cheek. He kisses me in the manner of a priest, and I get an impression of something round, like a Gouda cheese. He is unrecognizable. He looks like a jolly decent fat fellow. A man swept away by the torrent of fame who still likes to shake the hands of those on the riverbank. Prone to migraines. You feel that he considers headaches a waste of time. Short-sighted, he comes up close and peers at you to see how you have aged.

'Ah!' he says. 'So you still have an appetite twice a day? As for me, that pleasure has long gone. On the other hand, when my wife sees a salami on the table she sniffs the air, quivering with life. Come. Let us go and eat some soft-boiled eggs.' [. . .]

Now and then he winks almost imperceptibly. Hard to tell if it is a tic or a sign to his wife not to say too much, a signal of understanding.

The romantic looks in a wardrobe mirror and thinks it is the sea. The realist looks at the sea and thinks it is a wardrobe mirror. But the man who judges correctly says, in front of the mirror, 'This is a mirror,' and, in front of the sea, 'This is the sea.'

10 December.

A loose style – now there is charm.

The son of a peasant from this same village, who pushed a plough. My roots are still covered in earth.

The sun knitting pink clouds with its rays.

If there is something more unpleasant than ambition, it is a window-display of modesty.

As soon as you have looked it in the face, death is easy on the mind.

Now that I am mortally ill, I should like to make a few profound, historical utterances, which my friends will subsequently repeat; but then I start to get overexcited.

It is not exactly a sign from God that I am asking for. If for once I saw men act as they profess, my spirit would at once be moved.

To be ill for a whole year, so as to savour the tedium of it.

Before dying, I should like to make a quick trip around the world, one place after another. Yes, but wherever I found myself I'd have one of my migraines, so I would always be in the same place.

A coarse expression on the lips of a woman, like a slug on the petals of a rose.

To have reached an age where the death of others no longer surprises.

'Monsieur must have been handsome when he was young,' says the maid.

My death will not come as a surprise: it will come at the appointed time.

Now that I am ill, to every sentence I add the rider: 'If I live.'

The compulsion to observe is my illness. Almost as good as having a crime in the family.

My heart is a pendulum of cotton wool which now and then knocks lightly against its case.

The mind that is taking its leave – impossible to detain it. As if a dandelion were to try and hold on to its seeds.

Already, I am developing a taste for strolling in cemeteries.

The mystery of death is enough. All those other things one attaches to it are so many theatrical props.

Visit to the tomb of the Goncourts. In their pride, these men of letters did not lay claim to being men of letters. Two names, two dates: they thought that should suffice. Hah! But don't count on it.

Now that I am ill, my throat feels as if a snail is being boiled in it.

And that fellow who just passed me by, he looks ill too! It is the inverse of a ribbon. Back then I used to say: 'What! Him too?'

1910

22 January.

My heart beats like a buried miner who tries, by means of irregular knocking, to signal that he is still alive.

The detestable pleasure, almost in the nature of a tonic, of venting one's ill humour upon others.

All oak trees are historic, but some of them keep quiet about it.

Walk in the Bois. The old women one glimpses, buried in the depths of their carriages.

My name is on all the walls, on the posters of the *Paris-Journal*, but on the tramway not a soul knows me.

25 January.

The Paris flood. A lesser thing even than my impoverished imagination makes it out to be.

26 *January*.

Snow on water: silence upon silence.

27 *January*.

The flood. The most painful thing is the Gare St-Lazare. Things to be feared: lack of fresh water or fuel, and rats.

Odéon, thirty spectators. At the Théâtre Michel, where the floor is still soaked, people lifted their feet and amused themselves insofar as possible. But all of the theatres have received a body blow.

The 'Venice' atmosphere of the flood has disappeared. It is already merely tiresome.

16 February.

As absorbed as a cat watching on the ceiling the spokes of light from a lamp.

Now that I am ill, I can no longer put the key into the lock at the first go. It reminds me of one of my stories.

'I am grieving,' says Marinette. 'I am inconsolable. I would like to die.'

In my theatre I started from the principle that women are never unfaithful to men, and vice versa.

It is frightening how hard it is, when one is in good health, to take an interest in the misfortunes of others.

I cannot make up my mind whether to put an end to my troubles by calling upon God.

Yesterday, Descaves brought a Dr Crepel, who taps my chest, auscultates me gently, and uses a monitoring device – the same as that used by Renault – to take my blood pressure. It is normal: no hypertension. Nothing wrong with the heart, nothing wrong with the liver. Agrees more or less with Renault's findings, but persuades me to come to him for electrical treatment with high-frequency currents.

22 February.

Forty-six today. How much longer do I have? Until the autumn?

23 February.

Marinette weeps for the two of us, and, as for me, I help her a little.

I am starting to have bad nights, waiting for the final night.

Humour: modesty and wit combined. It is the everyday clothing of the mind. I have formed a high opinion, moral and literary, of humour.
Imagination leads us astray. Sensibility makes us dull.

In short, humour is Reason itself. Man regulated and corrected. No definition of it ever satisfied me.

Besides, everything is contained inside humour.

Is it because I was the last to enter the Académie Goncourt that I shall be the first to leave? A singular logic!

Yesterday, Fantec sounded my chest. We laughed like idiots as his ears wandered over my back. He had to start over again two or three times. Nothing in the lungs. The heart is distended. He could hear the valves galloping. That put an end to my laughter. Will the son pronounce the death sentence of the father?

Between my brain and me there is always a layer that I cannot penetrate.

To live while toying with death.

The man in the street does not know himself. He is capable of dying without any understanding of what made him tick. I speak literally, of the heart which beats in his breast. (As for the other kinds . . .) Man is as insensible as a watch.

6 March.

I do not understand life, but it's not impossible that God does, a little.

The apparent animation, the docile and resigned air of a weathercock.

15 March.

Whoever does not suffer morbidly from scruples should not even think of trying to be an honest man.

31 March.

Death of Moréas. Is it my turn?
He was a poet who betrayed his country, wrote a few good lines of verse, and took me for a fool.

6 April.

Last night, I tried to get up. Dead weight. A leg hanging outside. Then a trickle running down my leg. I let it reach my heel before I make up my mind not to bother. It will dry in the sheets, the way it did long ago, when I was Poil de Carotte.

[*Here the* Journal *breaks off. Jules Renard died on 22 May, 1910. Marinette died in 1938.*]